Merle Brown
Cairns, Australia
July 2001

KEY GUIDE

Australian
Palms, Ferns,
Cycads and Pandans

KEY GUIDE

Australian
Palms Ferns
Cycads and Pandans

Envirobook

Leonard Cronin

Illustrated by
Marion Westmacott

Leonard Cronin, is one of Australia's foremost natural history authors. Trained s a biologist, he is a prolific writer of books and articles on the Australian flora, fauna and the environment, bringing his own fascination with the natural world to the general reader. Among his other works are *The Australian Flora, The Australian Animal Atlas, Ancient Kingdoms and Natural Wonders, Koala, Presenting Australia's National Parks* and *The Illustrated Encyclopaedia of the Human Body.*

The illustrator of this volume, Marion Westmacott, is one of Australia's leading botanical illustrators. She works as a scientific illustrator at the Royal Botanic Gardens in Sydney.

First Published in Australia in 1989 by Reed Books
This edition first published in 2000 by Envirobook

Planned and produced by
Leonard Cronin Productions

Published in Australia by
Envirobook
38 Rose St, Annandale, NSW 2038

Copyright © Leonard Cronin, 1989
Key Guide is a registered trade mark

National Library of Australia Cataloguing-in-Publication Data:

Cronin, Leonard.
Key Guide to Australian Palms, Ferns, Cycads and Pandans

Bibliography
Includes index.

ISBN 0 85881 173 1

1. Palms, Ferns, Cycads, Pandans - Identification
1. Title (Series: Key Guides to Australian Flora)

584.5'0994

Publisher: Leonard Cronin
Design: Robert Taylor
Additional research: Gertrud Latour
Printer: Kyodo Printing Co, Singapore

Contents

Acknowledgements

Many people helped in the preparation of this book, and I would like to give special thanks to Ray Best, who supplied the majority of the reference material for the ferns from his extensive fern garden, and willingly gave of his time and expert knowledge; and to his knowledgeable and equally helpful wife, Marie. I would like to thank Alick Dockrill who gave me access to his large collection of native palms in Atherton; Karen and George Westmacott who helped with the photographic reference material; Beryl Geekie and Colin Harman who kindly supplied specimens of ferns; Esme Hoffman of O'Reilly's Guest House in Lamington National Park; the staff of Australia's excellent Botanical Gardens and Herbariums, in particular Anna Hallett, Tony Rodd and other staff members of the National Herbarium of NSW, without whose help this book would have been infinitely more difficult to produce. I would also like to thank the National Park Rangers and all those local experts who helped me on field expeditions. Special thanks to Robert Kooyman, and friends living on the beautiful north coast of NSW, who accompanied me on many field trips and helped to make this project such a pleasurable experience.

Preface
to the second edition

Introduction

Key Guide to Australian Palms, Ferns, Cycads and Pandans remains the only field guide to this beautiful and appealing section of the Australian flora. The first edition proved itself to be a popular reference work, and this new, updated edition incorporates changes to the scientific names, new information about distribution and new data where applicable.

Leonard Cronin, 2000.

This book is intended as a small step along the road to familiarisation with, and appreciation of the great diversity of plant life in Australia. It has been designed as a simple, easy to use field guide and introduction to some of the major and most commonly admired components of the rainforest flora: the palms and ferns. It also includes members of the interesting and unusual palm-like groups, the pandans and cycads, linked to the ferns and other ancient orders of seed-bearing plants by their mobile swimming sperm which require water to enable them to reach and fertilise the egg nucleus.

It is hoped that familiarity with some of the species described will help the reader to feel more at home in the Australian rainforests, and encourage further study of the less conspicuous and uncommon species, thus approaching a greater understanding of our place in the web of life on Earth.

It is far beyond the scope of this book to include all the species of palms, ferns, pandans and cycads in Australia. I have, however, aimed to describe those species more likely to be encountered by an interested observer. Some of these may be restricted to particular isolated habitats but are becoming popular in cultivation as more people take an interest in some of our more unusual and distinctive native species.

Classification of the palms and pandans is still in a period of flux, and much more fundamental work still has to be undertaken before all the species are defined. Those described here are all clearly identifiable and should pose few problems in their recognition. Allowance must, however, be made for variations due to soil types and habitat. Specimens growing at the limits of their range or in cultivation will often differ in their proportions, having

larger trunks and more luxuriant foliage when conditions are ideal, becoming smaller with sparser foliage in poor sites and habitats.

To my knowledge this is the first collection of colour paintings of the Australian pandans and cycads to appear in print, showing details of their fruit, the whole plant and its foliage; as well as illustrations of some of the lesser-known palms and the Native Banana, *Musa banksii*, sometimes mistaken for its cultivated counterpart. The illustrations by Marion Westmacott have been executed with style, accuracy and great patience to add a visual appeal to this book that photographs could not hope to match.

The visual key is designed to guide the reader to those pages of the book where species with similar, easily identifiable characteristics are grouped together. For example, all the ferns with pinnate fronds are grouped together, as are the palms with crownshafts, and those with fan-shaped fronds.

The information about each species is written to be as comprehensible and comprehensive as possible. The use of specialised botanical terminology has been kept to a minimum, and the information has been organised under sub-headings to be easily accessible, clearly relating to particular visible characteristics of the plant. The Latin names given are those currently accepted by the scientific community, those in parentheses are synonyms still to be found in the literature. Common names have been included because most people are more familiar with these and find the pronunciation of Latin names difficult.

We are the fortunate inhabitants of the greatest island continent on earth. A continent with a remarkably rich and diverse flora, allowed to flourish and evolve in isolation from the rest of the world by a series of geological upheavals that saw a portion of the ancient land of Gondwana marooned in the southern ocean, far away from the industrious and warring civilisations of the northern hemisphere.

That isolation ended two centuries ago when Europeans began to take over the guardianship of this country from the Aboriginal people. Dismayed and uncomfortable in a land so different from their origins, these new settlers attempted to change and modify their surroundings, hoping to recreate a land similar to their birthplaces.

Spurred on by developers, governments and industry we have penetrated the remotest regions of the Australian Continent, carving roads through our great rainforests to allow machines to tear down majestic trees left undisturbed by thousands of generations of people before us, while blindly crushing or displacing countless numbers of plants and animals that stand in their way. Many of these species are only found in our rapidly disappearing rainforests, the subject of so much debate not only in Australia but throughout the world. We live in the most environmentally destructive age in the history of mankind. We have the power and have demonstrated the will to virtually eradicate the Australian rainforests by the turn of the century.

We are not alone. In the last twenty years more than half the world's rainforests have been wiped off the face of the Earth. Science has finally conquered Nature. Where once stood mighty forests teeming with life we gaze out over vast plains carefully tended, sprayed and ploughed. True masters of the Earth we can walk without fear of predators or contact with plants and animals not to our liking.

The short term effects of this unchecked wholesale deforestation are becoming obvious even to the most myopic members of society: soil erosion at a level never before seen in the history of mankind; flooding caused by the removal of trees that bind the soil and hold the water from heavy rainfall; the proliferation of opportunistic weeds; the eradication of countless numbers of species of plants and animals; and the creation of mountains of waste paper products.

The long term effects will be nothing short of catastrophic and are only slowly being realised and accepted by the scientific community: warming of the planet through the build up of the so-called "greenhouse" gases such as carbon dioxide which is absorbed by trees and released by the burning of fossil fuel; alteration of the climate by the removal of trees; pollution of the waterways by modern farming practices; and a dramatic decrease in our resource base of biological material.

Most of these changes are irreversible. They are already beginning to make themselves felt, and nothing short of legislation will stem the tide of biological change that we have unleashed upon the planet; the legacies of which will be passed on to future generations who will judge us by our actions, and live or die with the consequences.

Rainforests are a finite source of materials offering very short term economic gains. If we continue to allow the timber companies and developers access to these areas then we will be assured a future without rainforests. Once cleared they will not regenerate without a massive input of human resources, an input that will far outweigh all the short term economic gains made by their destruction, at a cost to be borne by governments, and hence taxpayers. Such will be our legacy to our children.

But this is not all. We will lose the freedom to experience the primeval world. To visit a rainforest is to visit the cradle of life on Earth. About half the known plant species, a third of the Australian mammals and birds and a great diversity of our reptiles and insects have evolved and live in our rainforests. Despite this

knowledge rainforests remain, from a scientific point of view, relatively unknown. Many of the plant species have yet to be classified and described. Scientists know little about the ecology of rainforests, the interactions of the species, the food chains, the microclimates and habitats. Funding for this type of fundamental research is minimal. Governments are more comfortable pouring money into space research and high profile telecommunications and electronics projects than unravelling the complexities of life on earth. It is easier to bask in ignorance and continue to treat the environment and the forces of nature with contempt than pay for research into biological systems which will undoubtedly show the need for massive and quite fundamental changes to our industrial and environmental practices.

How to use this guide

To use this book you do not need any knowledge of plant classification. The following visual keys direct you to pages where plants with similar characteristics are gathered together.

Look at the specimen and compare the type of leaf with those described in the left hand columns of the Keys. Having found the nearest corresponding **General leaf shape**, look at the centre column and identify the closest **Form** of the plant. Now simply turn to the pages indicated in the right hand column and identify the plant by looking at the illustrations and descriptions given.

Example

Along the coast of central Queensland you come across a colony of tall palms growing along a creek at the edge of a small rainforest. They have feathery, dark green fronds atop a pale grey trunk with a prominent bright green crownshaft, and have masses of orange-red fruits hanging down below the crownshaft.

1. Using the keys you find the **Feather-leaved palms** in the left hand column resembles the **General leaf shape** of the palm.

2. In the centre column the **Palms with crownshaft** refers you to pages 14-36.

3. On page 16 you find that the illustration and description of the Bangalow Palm.

Palms and palm-like plants

General leaf shape	Form	Page

Feather-leaved palms

Palms with crownshaft — 14-36

Palms without crownshaft — 38-66

Climbing palms — 68-76

Fan-leaved palms — 78-100

Pandans — 102-112

Cycads — 114-122

Banana — 124

Ferns

General leaf shape	Form	Page

Simple
- Entire margins — 126
- Lobed margins — 126-130

Pinnate
- Entire margins — 132-134
- Indented margins — 134-148

Bipinnate
- Entire margins — 148-150
- Indented margins — 150-160

Tripinnate — 156-166

Tree ferns — 168-180

Illustrations and Descriptions

Archontophoenix alexandrae　　　　**Alexandra Palm**

The Alexandra Palm is a tall, slender, single-stemmed, feather-leaved palm of the tropical and subtropical rainforests of northeastern Australia. It has a prominent, smooth, pale-green crownshaft growing to 1 m long in mature specimens, topped by a medium-density crown of arching fronds with drooping leaflets with greyish undersurfaces.

Trunk Greenish-grey to grey, to 30 m high and 25 cm diameter, usually quite swollen at the base and prominently ringed with horizontal leaf scars. The commonly cultivated form *Beatriceae* has a very enlarged base and strongly indented, step-like leaf scars.

Leaves Fairly stiff, spreading and slightly twisted along the main axis; 2-3 m long and 60-90 cm broad. They are pinnately divided into numerous broad linear leaflets with entire, pointed tips, dark-green above and covered with minute silvery scales below. The leaflets are 30-45 cm long and 2-5 cm wide, evenly and closely spaced along the midrib of the leaf, forward pointing, angled upwards and arching gently. They have a prominent yellowish central vein which is raised on the upper surface, and conspicuous longitudinal veins below, giving the leaflets a slightly ridged appearance. The bases of the leaflets are quite constricted, with the margins folded down. The leaf stalk is short and smooth, mid-green, flat to concave above and convex below, with a wide, cylindrical, sheathing base that forms the crownshaft.

Inflorescence A large, much-branched panicle with many long, semi-pendulous, flower-bearing branchlets. It is 40-80 cm long with a stout, pale-yellow, flattened main stalk arising from the upper leaf scars on the trunk immediately below the crownshaft. Several inflorescences are often present at the same time. They are initially enclosed in 2 large pale-green to brown pointed, papery bracts, 30-45 cm long that fall before the flowers open.

Flowers White or cream and about 8 mm across. Male and female flowers are produced on the same inflorescence, typically in groups of 3, with one female between 2 males; or pairs of males only towards the ends of the branchlets of the inflorescence They have 3 sepals and 3 petals; the petals of the males just touch in bud and those of the females overlap. The males have 9-16 stamens and the females a single-celled ovary containing one ovule topped by a 3-lobed stigma.

Fruits Green turning red when ripe, ovoid, 10-15 mm long with a smooth waxy surface. They contain a single, elliptical, fibrous seed surrounded by a thin, fleshy layer with interlocking flattened longitudinal fibres running through it.

Habitat Naturally occurring along stream banks, in moist sheltered sites and swampy areas of coastal and near coastal tropical and subtropical rainforests, from sea level to about 1200 m, usually forming dense colonies. The fresh seeds germinate within 3 months and grow best in rich, well-drained soils in frost-free sites. They are quite hardy and will tolerate full sun.

Distribution Locally common from the Iron Range in the Cape York Peninsula in northeastern Qld to around Mackay. They are commonly cultivated and widely planted in parks and gardens as far south as Sydney, and are important in reducing erosion along stream banks.

Family Arecaceae.

Archontophoenix cunninghamiana

Bangalow Palm
Picabeen Palm

This graceful palm is a tall, single-stemmed, feather-leaved palm of the warm temperate and subtropical regions of eastern Australia. It has a prominent bright-green to rusty-brown crownshaft, 60 cm to 1 m long in mature specimens, topped by a relatively small, umbrella-shaped crown of long, curved, dark-green, twisted fronds.

Trunk Brown to greenish-grey turning pale grey when older, to 25 m high and 30 cm diameter, sometimes slightly swollen at the base, smooth and ringed with closely-spaced horizontal leaf scars.

Leaves Arch gently, 2-4 m long, pinnately divided into numerous, closely-spaced, opposite, slightly drooping leaflets, glossy dark-green on both surfaces. The leaflets are linear to lanceolate, 60-100 cm long and 3-8 cm wide in mature specimens, with long, pointed tips. They have a prominent raised yellow midvein on the upper surface and scattered large brown scales on the underside near the base. They are forward-pointing and emerge in a horizontal plane along either side of the midrib, which is twisted so that the terminal leaflets stand vertically. The margins are folded down to give the leaflets a constricted base. The leaf stalks are green with rusty brown scurf below, short and stout, 10-25 cm long and about 3-7 cm wide with wide, cylindrical, sheathing bases that surround the top of the trunk to form the crownshaft. New, unexpanded leaves form a vertical spike protruding above the crown.

Inflorescence A large, much-branched, fairly dense panicle, 90-150 cm long, with a short, thick, flattened, cream to pale-yellow main stalk and many long, slender, semi-pendulous flower-bearing branchlets. Several inflorescences are often present at the same time, arising from the upper leaf scars below the crownshaft. They are initially enclosed in 2 large, thin, pointed, papery bracts, 40-60 cm long, that fall before the flowers open.

Flowers Pale pink to pale lilac, stalkless, 3-5 mm across. Male and female flowers are produced on the same inflorescence, typically spirally arranged in irregular groups of 3, with one female between 2 males, and pairs of males only towards the ends of the branchlets. The female flowers are smaller, mature later than the males and only partially open. Both have 3 sepals and 3 petals; the petals overlap in the females and just touch in the male flower buds. Male flowers have 9-18 stamens fused into a disc at the base. Females have a 3-lobed stigma and a single-celled ovary containing one ovule.

Fruits Orange-red when ripe, ovoid to spherical, 10-15 mm across with a smooth, waxy surface and the pointed remains of the stigma at one end. They contain a single, elliptical, fibrous seed surrounded by a thin fleshy layer with a mesh of flattened fibres running through it.

Habitat Warm temperate to subtropical areas along stream banks, gullies and wet sites in rainforests, wet sclerophyll forests, rainforest margins, and in swampy areas in more open situations, to 700m, sometimes growing in large colonies. Fresh seed germinates within 6 months. The plants require well-drained soil, are quite hardy and can tolerate considerable exposure to sun and wind.

Distribution Locally common in coastal regions from around Mackay in central Qld to southeastern NSW near Bateman's Bay. They are commonly cultivated in parks and gardens as far south as Melbourne, and are important in reducing erosion on stream banks.

Family Arecaceae.

Carpentaria acuminata **Carpentaria Palm**

The Carpentaria Palm is a tall, slender, single-stemmed, feather-leaved palm of the tropical rain-forests of northern Australia. It has a smooth, greyish-green crownshaft, 60-100 cm long in mature specimens, bulging slightly at the base, and topped by a small, extended, widely spreading crown of arching fronds.

Trunk Greyish-green, to 30 m tall and 30 cm diameter, slightly swollen at the base and tapering gradually towards the top. It is smooth, ringed with leaf scars, and often covered by lichens.

Leaves Up to 4 m long, arching, with pendulous tips, pinnately divided into numerous, closely spaced, waxy leaflets, glossy dark-green above and slightly bluish-green below. The leaflets are narrow and strap-like, 20-60 cm long and 2-4 cm wide, tapering to an oblique, jagged tip with 2-4 teeth on the lower edge. The lower leaflets are broader with several ribs and more teeth. The terminal leaflets are united at their bases and fish-tail like. They are attached at an upward angle to the midrib with the edges of each leaflet folded down from the central vein. The leaf stalks are slender and about 30 cm long, slightly concave above and convex below. They are covered with whitish scales and have smooth margins and cylindrical sheathing bases that surround the trunk to form the crownshaft.

Inflorescence A large, semi-pendulous panicle to about 1.5 m long, with a stout, flattened stalk 10-20 cm long, and many slender, flower-bearing branches. Several inflorescences are often present at the same time and arise from the leaf scars below the crownshaft. They are enclosed by 2 broad, scoop-shaped sheathing bracts, 40-80 cm long, that fall before the flowers open.

Flowers White or cream, stalkless, about 1 cm across. Male and female flowers are produced on the same inflorescence, typically in groups of 3 with one female between 2 males, and males only in the upper part of the inflorescence. They have 3 petals and 3 sepals. Male flowers mature earlier than the females, and are slightly larger with about 30 stamens and narrow anthers opening in longitudinal slits to release the pollen grains. Females have a 3-lobed stigma and a single-celled ovary containing one ovule. Flowers are generally produced between September and January.

Fruits Scarlet when ripe with a yellow, cup-shaped calyx at the base. They are ovoid to spherical with a pointed tip, 1-2 cm long and 15-20 mm wide, comprising a thin smooth outer skin enclosing a thick, fleshy, juicy layer with straight black springy inner fibres, surrounding a single seed. They are ripe about 3 months after flowering, mainly from December to March.

Habitat Stream banks in low-lying, flood-prone sites in dense tropical rainforests, and in moist coastal monsoon vine thickets, sometimes forming small colonies, and often emerging from the surrounding canopy. The fresh seed germinates within 4 months, growing quite fast in hot, humid climates, preferring well-drained soil in sunny or shaded positions. They will grow further south although they are very frost tender.

Distribution Locally common in coastal regions of the NT from just southwest of Darwin to the King River, extending into the Melville Islands, the Coburg Peninsula and the Wessel Island Group. Commonly cultivated in parks, gardens and as a street tree in the tropics.

Family Arecaceae.

Gronophyllum ramsayi Northern Kentia Palm

The Northern Kentia Palm is a tall, single-stemmed, feather-leaved palm of the open forests of the far north of Australia and some adjacent islands. This little-known, robust palm has a yellowish-green crownshaft with a whitish bloom, 80-100 cm long in mature specimens and slightly swollen towards the centre, giving rise to a compact crown of greyish-green, strongly arching fronds with the leaflets held at an upright angle to the midrib.

Trunk Smooth, greenish-grey to grey, to 35 m tall and 35 cm diameter, slightly swollen around the middle and tapering towards the top. It is ringed with prominent dark leaf scars. Specimens have been found with branched trunks, with up to 5 stems emerging from the same point on the main trunk.

Leaves Up to 2.5 m long with a short, arching leaf stalk about 40-80 cm long, with smooth, spineless margins. They are pinnately divided into numerous closely and evenly spaced light green to blue-greyish green, linear leaflets, 30-90 cm long and 2-5 cm wide, tapering to a pointed tip. The leaf stalks are covered with a scurfy white material and have a long, sheathing base that encircles the trunk to form the crownshaft. The leaflets are forward-pointing and angled upwards on either side of the arching midrib to form a distinct V-shape.

Inflorescence A sparsely-branched, pendulous panicle about 30-50 cm long with a short, thick, flattened, arching stalk, forked twice into a brush-like structure with drooping, flower-bearing branchlets. Several inflorescences are often present at the same time, arising from the leaf scars at the base of the crownshaft. They are enclosed in the bud stage by 2 large, thin bracts that are shed before the flowers open.

Flowers Creamy-white, about 6 mm across. Separate male and female flowers are produced on the same inflorescence They are typically arranged in groups of 3 with one female between 2 males. The males have 3 pointed sepals, 3 petals with the edges touching in bud, 6-12 stamens and a minute, 3-lobed sterile pistil. Female flowers have 3 rounded sepals, 3 petals overlapping at the base, a single-celled ovary containing one ovule and a simple stigma. Flowers are mainly produced from July to October.

Fruits Yellow to brown or bright, waxy red when ripe, 12-15 mm long and 7-8 mm wide, ovoid to egg-shaped with the pointed remains of the stigma at one end. They have a single, hard-shelled seed surrounded by a thin, oily, fleshy outer layer. Fruits generally ripen from September to February.

Habitat Naturally occurring in deep, sandy soil in tall, moist, eucalypt forests, sandstone cliffs and flat sites subject to flooding, where they usually form extensive colonies. The fresh seed germinates sporadically in 6-12 months. The seedlings are slow-growing, easy to transplant at an early stage, very cold sensitive, and prefer well-drained soil with plenty of available water. They are quite hardy and can tolerate considerable exposure to the sun.

Distribution Scattered in western Arnhem Land, Kakadu National Park and the Cobourg Peninsula in the NT, and some of the nearby islands, including Croker and Melville Islands.

Family Arecaceae.

Hedyscepe canterburyana   **Umbrella Palm**

The Umbrella Palm is a sturdy, medium-sized, single-stemmed, feather-leaved palm growing on the mountains of Lord Howe Island in elevated, cloud-covered sites. This is a very handsome palm with a bulbous, bluish-green to greyish-green crownshaft, 80-100 cm long in mature specimens, topped by a compact crown of some 7-8 stiff, dark-green, arching fronds with erect, upward-pointing leaflets.

Trunk Green turning grey, 4-10 m tall and 9-18 cm diameter. It is straight and smooth with a slightly bulging base and ringed with prominent, closely-spaced oblique or horizontal leaf scars.

Leaves Up to 3 m long with a stiff, arching and slightly twisted midrib and a short, stout, greyish-green to brownish-green stalk. They are pinnately divided into numerous stiff, closely and evenly spaced, forward-pointing leaflets, dark-green on both surfaces, attached at an upward angle to the midrib of the frond to form a distinct V-shape. The leaflets are 20-30 cm long and 2-4 cm wide, lanceolate with long pointed tips and 3 or more prominent, raised, yellow main veins. The margins are curved down at the base. The leaf stalks are concave above and convex below, with large sheathing bases that encircle the top of the trunk to form the crownshaft.

Inflorescence A much-branched, pendulous panicle, 20-40 cm long with a short, stout, flattened stalk and fairly stiff, fleshy, flower-bearing branchlets. Several inflorescences are usually present at the same time. They arise from the upper leaf scars on the trunk at the base of the crownshaft, and are initially enclosed in 2 pointed, flattened bracts that fall before the flowers open.

Flowers Yellow to orange-yellow, about 1 cm across. Both male and female flowers are borne on the same inflorescence, they both have 3 narrow sepals and 3 angled petals, their edges overlapping in the budding female flowers, and touching in the male flowers. The males have 9-12 stamens, while the females have 3 sterile stamens.

Fruits Large, smooth, shiny green turning deep-red to brownish when ripe, ovoid, 4-5 cm long, stalkless with the pointed remains of the stigma at the end. They comprise a single seed enclosed in a thin, fleshy layer, and take 3-4 years to mature.

Habitat Naturally occurring in elevated areas from 400-900 m in moist montane forests and on cliffs, where they are subject to low cloud and high winds. Fresh seed germinates erratically over 12 months, and grows best in rich, well-drained soil with partial shade and moist conditions. They are slow growing and prefer shady sites when young. They will tolerate mild frosts, and prefer cool nights and temperate conditions.

Distribution Endemic to Lord Howe Island, although they are cultivated in parks and gardens in temperate Australia as far south as Melbourne.

Family Arecaceae.

Hydriastele wendlandiana

This delicate palm is a medium-sized to tall, very slender, clumping, feather-leaved species of the tropical rainforests of northern and northeastern Australia, usually with 2-4 dominant trunks and a number of suckers around the base. It has a slender, whitish-green crownshaft, 40-60 cm long in mature specimens, topped by a sparse crown of 6-7 upward-pointing fronds with fish-tail shaped terminal leaflets.

Trunk Grey, 7-15 m tall and 6-12 cm diameter, straight, smooth and ringed with relatively widely-spaced, prominent, horizontal leaf scars.

Leaves Up to 2 m long with a short stalk 20-50 cm long. They are pinnately divided into 30-50 fairly thin, irregularly-spaced, unequal leaflets, dull, pale to dark-green on both surfaces. They emerge at an upward-pointing angle to the midrib, giving the frond a V-shape. The leaflets are 20-60 cm long and 2-10 cm wide, linear to oblong with oblique, jagged or toothed tips, a prominent yellowish central vein and a number of raised parallel veins. The terminal leaflets are much shorter and joined at their bases to give a fish-tail appearance to the end of the frond. The leaf stalks are convex below and covered with brown or whitish scurf, flat or slightly concave above, with a wide, sheathing, cylindrical base that encircles the top of the trunk to form the crownshaft.

Inflorescence Usually 30-35 cm long, comprising a very short, flattened stalk, divided into a number of semi-erect to pendulous, unbranched, slender, wiry, pale brown, flower-bearing branches. Several inflorescences are often present at the same time, arising from the upper leaf scars at the base of the crownshaft. They are initially enclosed in 2 large, thin, pale-brown, papery bracts which are shed before the fruits ripen.

Flowers Pale yellow or greenish, about 8 mm across with 3 sepals and 3 petals joined for half their length in the female flowers. Both sexes are produced on the same inflorescence, typically arranged in groups of 3 along the branches with one female between 2 males. The males have 6 stamens, while the females have a single-celled ovary and a small, 3-lobed stigma. Flowering from July to November.

Fruits Bright red when ripe, ovoid to globular with longitudinal ridges, about 1 cm long and 5-8 mm across, comprising a single, hard-shelled seed surrounded by a thin, fleshy and fibrous outer layer. They are produced in pendulous spikes and ripen from October to January.

Habitat Naturally occurring in open swampy areas, along streams, and in moist sites in closed tropical rainforests and rainforest margins. Young plants usually require shade, whereas mature trees often have their crowns exposed to full sun. The fresh seed germinates in 3-12 months and the plants require well-drained, rich soil and plenty of water. They are quite slow growing and very sensitive to the cold.

Distribution Widespread and locally common in coastal areas of the NT and northeastern Qld, from the tip of Cape York and some Torres Strait islands to just south of Tully. They are not widely cultivated, but will grow well in subtropical areas.

Family Arecaceae.

Normanbya normanbyi   **Black Palm**

The Black Palm is a tall, slender, single-stemmed, feather-leaved palm of the lowland tropical rain-forests of northeastern Australia. This attractive palm has a distinctive, whitish-grey crownshaft, 50-100 cm long in mature specimens, slightly swollen at the base, and gives rise to a graceful, relatively dense crown of 9-12 arching, plume-like fronds.

Trunk Light grey to greyish green, to 20 m tall and 20 cm diameter, swollen at the base with vertical cracks, and tapering gradually towards the top. It is smooth and hard with fine vertical corrugations, and ringed with prominent horizontal leaf scars.

Leaves Up to 3 m long with an arching midrib and short, stout leaf stalk, 15-60 cm long. The leaves are pinnately divided into numerous wedge-shaped leaflets, shiny dark-green above, dull and paler-green to bluish-white below, with toothed or notched tips. The leaflets are often arranged in groups of 2 or more in mature plants, attached at their bases at many angles around the midrib of the leaf to give the frond a distinctly feathery appearance. They are 30-45 cm long and 10-35 mm wide, with 2-3 prominent main veins. In young plants the leaflets are solitary and attached at either side of the midrib in the same plane. The leaf stalks are convex below and covered with mealy white hairs, with a wide cylindrical sheathing base that encircles the top of the trunk to form the crownshaft.

Inflorescence A large, pendulous, much branched panicle to about 50 cm long, with a short, flattened stalk. It is initially enclosed in 2 tubular bracts, 15-30 cm long, which are shed when the flowers open. Several inflorescences are often present at the same time, arising from the upper leaf scars below the crownshaft.

Flowers Cream or white, about 15 mm across, spirally arranged in large clusters on the branchlets of the inflorescence Male and female flowers are produced on the same inflorescence. They are typically arranged with one female between 2 males on the lower parts of the branchlets, with solitary or paired males only on the upper parts. The males have numerous stamens with pink anthers and a sterile pistil. The females have a single-celled ovary containing one ovule and 3 small, sterile stamens.

Fruits Deep pink to scarlet or purplish-brown when ripe, ovoid to pear-shaped, with a point at one end. They are about 4 cm long and 3 cm across, comprising a large, ovoid, roughly-ridged seed surrounded by a fleshy layer containing many straight fibres.

Habitat Naturally occurring in dense tropical rainforests to about 500 m altitude in high rainfall districts near streams and swampy areas, mainly in gravelly alluvial soils, often forming scattered colonies. Fresh seed usually germinates within 3 months, and the plants prefer rich, well-drained soil in warm, frost-free sites.

Distribution Endemic to coastal areas of far northeastern Qld from Mossman to Mt Amos on the Cape York Peninsula. They are cultivated in tropical and subtropical regions, and grow successfully in warm coastal areas as far south as Sydney.

Family Arecaceae.

Ptychosperma bleeseri

This little-known species is a medium-sized, very slender, clumping, feather-leaved palm of the moist tropical forests of the far north of Australia. It has 2-3 main stems and a number of suckers around the base, and a relatively small, open crown of only 3-6 stiff, arching fronds, the upper ones standing erect and the lower ones horizontal and drooping. The fronds arise from a distinct pale-green crownshaft.

Trunk Green, becoming brownish-grey, smooth, to 10 m tall and about 3-5 cm diameter, wider at the base, tapering gradually towards the top, and ringed with relatively widely-spaced, prominent leaf scars. The trunk is weak and often supported by surrounding trees. In poor sites it bends under the weight of the crown and may become semi-prostrate.

Leaves Up to 1.5 m long, stiff, with an arching midrib and a relatively short, slender, pale-green leaf stalk, 10-20 cm long, concave above and convex below with a cylindrical sheathing base that forms the crownshaft. The leaves are pinnately divided into 30-40 broad, forward-pointing leaflets, mid-green above and slightly paler below, evenly spaced at a slight upward angle along the midrib, forming a shallow V-shape. The leaflets are 20-38 cm long and 2-5 cm wide, broad-linear to wedge-shaped with oblique to concave, notched or toothed tips, a narrow base, and margins curved downwards. They have a prominent raised midvein on the upper surface and thickened marginal veins. The terminal leaflets are united at their bases and fish-tail like.

Inflorescence A sparsely-branched, semi-pendulous panicle, 20-35 cm long, comprising a short, thick, flattened, yellowish-brown stalk about 5 cm long, giving rise to several branches and divided again into small flower-bearing branchlets. The inflorescence is initially sheathed by 2 large overlapping greenish bracts about 30 cm long that fall before flowering. Several inflorescences are often present at the same time, arising from the upper leaf scars at the base of the crownshaft.

Flowers White to creamy-yellow, about 6 mm long with 3 overlapping sepals and petals. Both sexes are produced on the same inflorescence, arranged in scattered irregular clusters, typically in groups of 3 with one female between 2 males, and pairs of males only towards the ends of the branchlets. The males open first, and have numerous long, protruding stamens; the females have a single-celled ovary containing one ovule, and 3 stigmas.

Fruits Bright red when ripe, ovoid with a short point at the tip, 12-18 mm long and 8-12 mm across. They contain a large, single, shelled seed with 5 longitudinal ridges, surrounded by a soft, thin, fleshy and fibrous layer.

Habitat Naturally occurring in scattered colonies in dense rainforest around the margins of freshwater swamps and permanent lowland freshwater creeks. The fresh seed germinates in 2-6 months, and requires rich, well-drained soil. They will tolerate full sun, but are better in shady sites.

Distribution Localised and rare in coastal regions of the NT, particularly near Darwin in threatened, isolated rainforest pockets including Koolpinyah and Black's Jungle.

Family Arecaceae.

Ptychosperma elegans

Solitaire Palm

The Solitaire Palm is a tall, slender, single-stemmed, feather-leaved palm of the moist tropical rainforests of northeastern Australia. This is a very distinctive species with a relatively small crown of only 6-8 stiff, arching fronds, the upper ones standing erect and the lower ones horizontal and drooping. The fronds arise from a short green crownshaft covered with a whitish scurf, 50-65 cm long with a slightly bulbous base.

Trunk Usually green and smooth towards the top, becoming rough and grey with small vertical fissures on the lower part. The trunk grows to 15 m tall and 7-20 cm diameter, is slightly swollen at the base and tapers gradually towards the top. It is ringed with relatively widely-spaced, prominent, step-like horizontal leaf scars.

Leaves Up to 2.5 m long, stiff, with an arching midrib and a relatively short, yellowish-green leaf stalk, 10-30 cm long, concave above and convex below with a cylindrical sheathing base that forms the crownshaft. The leaves are pinnately divided into 40-60 broad, forward-pointing leaflets, dark-green above and slightly paler below, evenly spaced at a slight upward-pointing angle along the midrib. The leaflets are 40-80 cm long and 3-11 cm wide, broad-lanceolate with oblique, notched tips and a narrow base with the margins curved downwards. They have a prominent raised midvein on the upper surface and thickened marginal veins. The terminal leaflets are united at their bases and fish-tail like.

Inflorescence A much-branched, semi-pendulous panicle, 30-60 cm long, comprising a short, thick, flattened, green stalk, giving rise to several branches and divided again into numerous flower-bearing branchlets. The inflorescence is initially sheathed by 2 large overlapping greenish bracts, 30-50 cm long, that fall before flowering. Several inflorescences are often present at the same time, arising from the upper leaf scars at the base of the crownshaft.

Flowers White and fragrant, about 8 mm across, with 3 overlapping sepals and petals. Both sexes are produced on the same inflorescence, arranged in scattered irregular clusters, typically in groups of 3 with one female between 2 males, and pairs of males only towards the ends of the branchlets. The males open first, and have 30 or more long, protruding stamens, while the female flowers have a single-celled ovary containing one ovule, and 3 stigmas.

Fruits Bright red when ripe, ovoid to egg-shaped, 14-18 mm long and 12-14 mm across. They contain a large, single seed with 5 longitudinal grooves surrounded by a soft, thin, fleshy and fibrous layer.

Habitat Naturally occurring in scattered colonies in lowland tropical rainforests, where they are found in sheltered gullies and ridges in high rainfall areas. The fresh seed germinates within 6 months and the plants prefer rich, well-drained soil and shady sites when young. They are relatively fast growing and the older plants will tolerate full sun but not frosts.

Distribution Locally common in coastal regions of northeastern Qld from the Iron Range in the Cape York Peninsula to Mackay. They are commonly cultivated in parks and gardens as far south as Sydney.

Family Arecaceae.

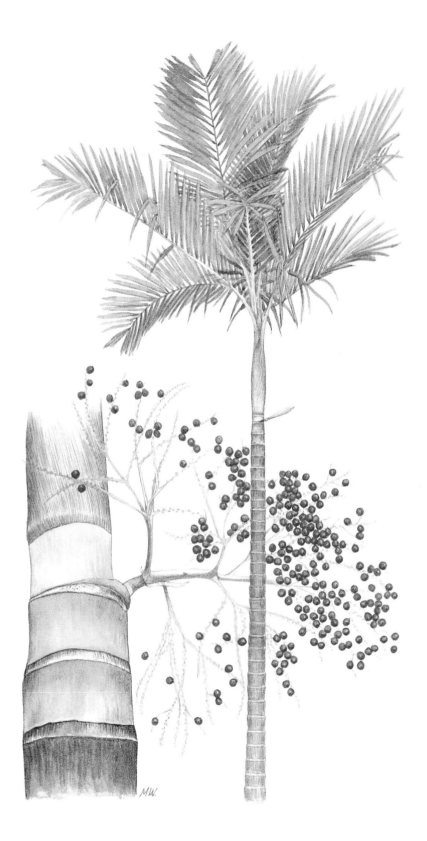

Ptychosperma macarthurii   **Macarthur Palm**

The Macarthur Palm is a small to medium-sized, single-stemmed or clumping, feather-leaved palm, confined to moist lowland forests in the northeastern tip of Australia, and extending into New Guinea. This compact palm usually grows as an understorey species with up to 20 slender trunks forming a dense clump. It has a loose crown of 7-10 shiny-green arching fronds with broad, blunt leaflets arising from a light green crownshaft, 40-70 cm long, slightly bulging at the base, and pale purplish in parts.

Trunk Greenish-grey, smooth, to 8 m tall and 4-10 cm diameter, tapering from the base, and ringed with prominent, widely-spaced leaf scars.

Leaves Up to 3 m long with a green slender stalk, 30-50 cm long, concave above and convex below with a long, sheathing base that surrounds the top of the trunk to form the crownshaft. The leaves are pinnately divided into 30-60 irregularly-spaced leaflets, shiny-green on both surfaces, arising in a horizontal plane on either side of the arching midrib. The leaflets are 30-60 cm long and 4-10 cm wide, oblong to wedge-shaped with oblique, irregularly toothed, flattened tips, a raised yellow midvein on the upper surface and thickened marginal veins. They have a constricted base with the margins folded down. The terminal leaflets are shorter and fused at their bases to give a fish-tail appearance to the end of the leaf.

Inflorescence A sparsely-branched panicle, 20-80 cm long with a green, turning pale-yellow, flattened stalk about 3 cm wide at the base. Several inflorescences may be present at the same time, arising from the upper leaf scars below the crownshaft. They are initially enclosed in 2 large overlapping cream to yellowish bracts, 15-40 cm long, that fall before the flowers open. The long, flower-bearing branchlets become pendulous under the weight of the fruit.

Flowers Greenish-yellow to cream and ovoid. Male flowers are about 8 mm long, and females about 3 mm long. Both are produced on the same inflorescence, although the female flowers develop when the males are falling. They are typically arranged in clusters of 3 with one female between 2 males on the lower parts of the branchlets, and pairs of males only in the upper parts. Both have 3 petals and 3 sepals, while the males have up to 100 white stamens and an elongated sterile pistil, and the females a single celled ovary with one ovule, 3 stigmas and minute, sterile stamens.

Fruits Green turning bright-red when ripe, waxy, egg-shaped, 12-15 mm long with a pointed tip. They have a fleshy and fibrous outer coat with a slightly acid taste, surrounding a single seed with 5 deep longitudinal grooves. Fruits are stalkless and borne in long, pendulous clusters.

Habitat Naturally occurring in moist tropical lowland forests and rainforests, mostly as understorey plants, forming localised colonies among other palms and large trees along creek banks and the margins of freshwater swamps. Fresh seed germinates in 2-3 months. The plants are tolerant of full sun, but are cold-sensitive and prefer rich, well-drained soil in a warm location protected from drying winds.

Distribution Restricted to central and northern parts of the Cape York Peninsula in Qld and extending into New Guinea. They are widely cultivated in the tropics, and will grow as far south as Sydney in protected sites.

Family Arecaceae.

Rhopalostylis baueri **Norfolk Palm**

The Norfolk Palm is a medium-sized, fairly robust, single-stemmed, feather-leaved palm native to the lowland forests of Norfolk Island. This distinctive palm has a prominent, bulging green crownshaft about 50 cm long, thinly covered with brown scurfy material, and topped by a compact, erect crown of stiff, slightly arching fronds with some drooping leaflets.

Trunk Green turning brownish-grey to grey in older specimens, 10-16 m tall and 12-30 cm diameter. The trunk is smooth and straight with a slightly bulging base and ringed with closely spaced, prominent, horizontal leaf scars.

Leaves Up to 4 m long with a very short green stalk and a stout midrib, both with a brownish scurfy material below. The leaves are pinnately divided into numerous closely-spaced, forward-pointing leaflets, dark-green on both surfaces, attached at an upward angle to the midrib of the frond to form a shallow V-shape. The leaflets are 80-100 cm long and 2-3 cm wide, fairly stiff and erect, slightly arching, linear to lanceolate with pointed tips, often shredded by the wind, and with a number of prominent raised longitudinal veins. The under surfaces of the leaflets and their main veins are sprinkled with small brown scales, and their margins are turned downwards at the narrow base. Young plants have a reddish tinge to the leaves. The leaf stalk has a large sheathing base that completely encircles the trunk to form the crownshaft.

Inflorescence A semi-pendulous, much-branched panicle to about 1 m long, with a short, thick, flattened stalk. Several inflorescences are often present at the same time, arising from the upper leaf scars on the trunk below the crownshaft once the palm has reached a height of about 1.5 m. They are initially enclosed in 2 short, broad, pale-brown or cream interlocking bracts that fall as the flowers begin to open.

Flowers White to pale-mauve and very crowded on the branchlets of the inflorescence. They are typically arranged in groups of 3 with one female between 2 males, and pairs of males only towards the ends of the branchlets. Male flowers have 3 narrow sepals and 3 keeled, spreading petals with their edges touching in bud, 6 stamens and a conspicuous, sterile, cylindrical pistil. The females are shorter with 3 sepals and 3 overlapping petals in bud, a single-celled ovary and a 3-lobed stigma.

Fruits Green turning scarlet-red when ripe, spherical to ovoid, about 12 mm diameter, comprising a single seed clothed in longitudinal fibres and surrounded by a thin fleshy and fibrous layer.

Habitat Naturally occurring in dense lowland forests close to the sea in a warm temperate climate with a plentiful supply of water. Fresh seed germinates readily within 3 months and the plants prefer moist, shady sites in temperate areas.

Distribution Locally common in remnant forests of Norfolk Island, but cultivated in temperate areas of Australia in parks and gardens from Melbourne to Brisbane.

Family Arecaceae.

Wodyetia bifurcata

Foxtail Palm

The Foxtail Palm is a medium-sized, single-stemmed, feather-leaved palm of the open woodlands of far northeastern Australia. This elegant species has a long, pale-green crownshaft with a whitish bloom, slightly swollen at the base, 80-120 cm long, topped by a graceful, widely-spreading crown of 6-10 light green, plume-like fronds.

Trunk Light-grey to brownish-grey, slightly swollen towards the middle and at the base, 6-20 m tall and 20-25 cm diameter. The trunk is smooth and hard with fine vertical corrugations and ringed with relatively widely-spaced horizontal leaf scars.

Leaves Up to 3.2 m long with an arching midrib and short, stout leaf stalk. The leaves are pinnately divided into numerous oblong-elliptic to wedge-shaped leaflets, glossy light-green above, dull and paler below with a whitish sheen. They have ragged, toothed or notched tips, are regularly arranged along the midrib and mostly cut to their bases to form many narrow, linear or wedge-shaped segments, radiating around the midrib to give the frond a feathery appearance. The leaflets are 45-79 cm long and 2-5 cm wide with a number of prominent yellow veins. The central leaflets are divided into 11-17 segments with ribbed margins, while the terminal leaflets are entire or divided into 2-4 segments. The leaf stalk is 29-42 cm long and about 5 cm wide, flattish above and convex below, green with white to brownish scales and a cylindrical sheathing base that encircles the top of the trunk to form the crownshaft.

Inflorescence A large, straight to pendulous, much-branched panicle, 75-112 cm long with a flattened stalk. A number of inflorescences are usually present at the same time, arising from the upper leaf scars below the crownshaft. They are enclosed in bud by 2 tubular bracts about 60 cm long, which are shed when the flowers open.

Flowers Creamy-green, with both male and female flowers produced on the same inflorescence. They usually grow in groups of 3 with one female between 2 males on the lower parts of the branchlets, and solitary or paired males only on the upper parts. Male flowers are about 15 mm across with many stamens, and the females are about 1 cm across with a single-celled ovary containing one ovule, and 3 short stigmas.

Fruits Orange-red when ripe, ovoid to globular with a pointed tip, 5-6 cm long and 3-4 cm across. Each fruit comprises a single, cylindrical seed about 3 cm long surrounded by a fleshy and fibrous outer layer.

Habitat Naturally occurring in open woodlands with some rainforest species, from sea-level into the low ranges, to about 400 m altitude. They grow in prolific stands along creeks on granite soils among large boulders. The fresh seed usually germinates in 2-3 months, and the seedlings can be transplanted at an early stage, although they have a deep root system. They can tolerate full sun and dry climates, but need plenty of water.

Distribution Confined to the Melville Range near Bathurst Bay on the Cape York Peninsula of northeastern Qld.

Family Arecaceae.

Seeds boiled for hallucinatory reasons!

Syagruf romanzoffianum   Queen Palm

The Queen Palm is a tall, robust, single-stemmed, feather-leaved palm, endemic to the coastal forests of Brazil, but widely planted in Australia and naturalised in parts of Queensland. This fast-growing species lacks a crownshaft, and the dark-green, arching, feathery fronds form a wide, spreading crown, often with a number of dead fronds hanging from the top of the trunk.

Trunk Grey, to 20 m tall and 30-60 cm diameter, straight or sometimes swollen at the base or about half way up. The trunk is smooth with large, widely-spaced horizontal leaf scars.

Leaves Up to 5 m long with a stout, arching stalk about 1 m long. They are pinnately divided into numerous crowded leaflets, dark-green on both surfaces, often arranged in small groups, and attached at different angles around the midrib, giving the leaf a plume-like appearance. The leaflets are narrow-linear, to 1 m long and 3 cm wide, with a long, pointed tip. They are soft and drooping with turned-down margins at the base and a prominent central vein, raised on the upper surface. The leaf stalk is dark-green and deeply concave above, convex below and covered with white scurf when young. The leaves have large, bulbous, purplish brown or whitish bases with shredded fibrous margins wrapped around the top of the trunk.

Inflorescence A much-branched panicle, 1-2 m long, with a short, stout stalk and numerous slender, flower-bearing branchlets. Several inflorescences are often present at the same time, arising from the base of the lower leaves within the crown. They are initially enclosed in 2 pointed, woody bracts that split open to release the flowers and remain attached to the base of the inflorescence for some time.

Flowers Yellow and typically in groups of 3, with one female between 2 males in the central part of the branchlets, and pairs of males only in the upper parts. The male flowers are 8-10 mm long, and the females about 5 mm long. They have 3 sepals and 3 petals; the males have 6 stamens and the females a 3-celled ovary with a 3-lobed stigma.

Fruits Are green turning yellow when ripe, broad-ovoid with a pointed tip, 25-30 mm long and 2-3 cm wide. The seeds are globular and surrounded by a fleshy and fibrous outer layer. They are crowded into a large pendulous mass, and sought after by fruit bats.

Habitat Naturally occurring in forested areas along river banks and near the coast, where they often form very large stands. Fresh seed germinates irregularly and takes about 2 months in warm conditions. They are fast growing, will tolerate salt-laden winds and are easy to transplant, preferring plenty of water, loamy soil and filtered sunlight.

Distribution Native to South America, they are very commonly planted in Australia and have become naturalised in parts of Queensland, growing in both inland and coastal areas from the tropics to temperate regions as far south as Melbourne. They are commonly cultivated as indoor plants.

Family Arecaceae.

Arenga australasica

A tall, clumping, feather-leaved palm of the coastal rainforests of northeastern Australia and the adjacent islands, this species usually has 1-3 dominant stems and numerous suckers around the base. The fronds are widely-spaced along the trunk, which lacks a crownshaft.

Trunk Light grey, to 20 m tall and 30 cm diameter. Younger stems are covered with thick, papery, fibrous tissue, and retain the black, fibrous remains of the old leaf bases. These are gradually shed to leave a smooth surface ringed with prominent, widely-spaced leaf scars.

Leaves Broadly ovate in outline, up to 3.5 m long, with a stout, cylindrical, rough-textured leaf stalk to 1.6 m long. The leaves are pinnately divided into closely-spaced linear leaflets, to 1 m long and 7 cm wide, glossy dark-green above and covered with a whitish scurf below. They have a prominent midvein raised on the lower surface, irregularly notched jagged tips with the notches often extending down the margins, broad bases with the margins folded upwards, and often a small, yellowish, ear-like lobe at the attachment point. The leaflets are stiff and spreading, drooping when older, grouped in small clusters pointing upwards to form a very shallow V-shape, or radiating around the upper side of the midrib, particularly near the base of the frond. The terminal leaflets are fused at their bases and fish-tail like. The leaf stalk is covered with whitish scurf and has dark-brown to black fibrous margins at the base, and expands to partially sheath the trunk.

Inflorescence An arching panicle, 1-2 m long, with a drooping tip and numerous long, thin, green, pendulous, flower-bearing branchlets. Inflorescences arise from the leaf bases and are covered with several papery bracts that fall as the flowers open. The first inflorescences are produced among the upper leaves and progressively appear down the trunk. When the lowest has produced its fruit the trunk dies, to be replaced by another sucker from the rootstock. Only a single mature palm in the clump flowers at any one time.

Flowers Yellow and about 1 cm across. Both male and female flowers are borne on the same inflorescence, typically arranged in groups of 3 with one female between 2 males. They have 3 sepals, overlapping in the males, and 3 petals, joined at the base in the females. The males have 6 or more stamens, while the females have a 2-3 celled ovary and a 3-lobed stigma.

Fruits Scarlet when ripe, globular, stalkless, about 2 cm across, containing 2-3 seeds with very hard, smooth coats, embedded in a fleshy outer layer that contains a highly irritating caustic juice. They ripen sporadically.

Habitat Stony creek beds on sandy or red basalt soils in near-coastal and littoral rainforests, usually in partial shade. They are very sensitive to cold conditions and are poorly represented in cultivation. The fresh seed germinates erratically over 2-12 months, or longer.

Distribution Coastal districts of northeastern Qld from Cooktown to Tully, and some offshore islands adjacent to northern Qld and the NT, where they are more common.

Family Arecaceae.

Caryota rumphiana   **Fishtail Palm**

The Fishtail Palm is a tall, slender, single-stemmed, bipinnate-leaved palm confined to the lowland monsoonal rainforests of northeastern Australia, and extending into New Guinea, and South-East Asia. This highly ornamental species lacks a crownshaft, the arching, bipinnate fronds with fishtail-shaped leaflets are quite widely spaced along the trunk and form a very attractive spreading crown extending a considerable way below the apex of the trunk.

Trunk Grey, to about 20 m tall and 30-40 cm diameter, tapering gradually from the base. It has small vertical fissures and is ringed with widely-spaced leaf scars. The upper part of the trunk is wrapped in layers of fibre and the papery, persistent remains of the leaf bases.

Leaves Grow to between 3 and 7 m long and about 3 m across, with a cylindrical stalk to 1 m long. They are bipinnately divided into numerous widely-spaced, thick and leathery segments, bright green on both surfaces. The leaf segments are 10-40 cm long and 5-8 cm wide, stalkless, wedge-shaped or fan-shaped with numerous veins radiating from their constricted bases to the ragged, irregularly-toothed tips, some of which have slender, blunt points. The leaf stalk is green with patches of small brown scales, and partially sheathes the trunk with its wide base and black, fibrous margins. The main axis arches slightly, while the lateral stalks and the leaf segments droop.

Inflorescence A large panicle, 1-3 m long, with a stout stalk about 60 cm long bearing numerous pendulous, flower-bearing branchlets, sheathed in bud by several overlapping, thin-textured bracts. The inflorescences are produced only at maturity. Beginning at the top of the palm, they arise from each successive lower leaf axil over a period of 5-7 years. The plant dies when the fruit from the lowest inflorescence matures.

Flowers Mauve in bud, becoming white or cream. They are 10-15 mm across with 3 small sepals and 3 rounded petals. The edges of the petals of the female buds overlap, while those of the males just touch. Both sexes are produced by the same plant in groups of 3 on the branchlets of the inflorescence, typically with one female between 2 males. The males have more than 30 stamens; the females a single ovary with 2-3 cells each containing one ovule, and a 3-lobed stigma.

Fruits Dark purple to black, 25-30 mm across, hard and globular with 1 (rarely 2) seeds with a thick, hard seed coat surrounded by a thick fleshy layer which contains highly irritating, needle-like, oxalate crystals, covered by a tough outer skin. The seeds must be handled carefully as they produce an intense burning sensation, although they are eaten by cassowaries.

Habitat Naturally occurring along stream banks in wet tropical rainforests, forming scattered colonies with individuals at various stages of maturity. Fresh seed germinates within 6-12 months, and the palms require rich, well-drained soil in frost-free, shady sites, with plenty of water during dry periods.

Distribution Confined to lowland areas of the Cape York Peninsula in northeastern Qld, extending to New Guinea, Indonesia, the Philippines and Malaysia. They are not commonly cultivated, although they will grow in warm temperate areas as far south as Sydney.

Family Arecaceae.

Cocos nucifera   **Coconut Palm**

The Coconut Palm is a tall, slender, single-stemmed, feather-leaved palm, naturalised on the beaches of tropical Australia and adjacent islands. This classically beautiful palm lacks a crownshaft and has a dense, roughly ovoid crown of bright green, stiff, slightly arching fronds with drooping leaflets. A number of cultivars exist, varying from the typical tall, slender tree to dwarf varieties with fruits of various sizes, shapes and colours.

Trunk Grey, to 35 m tall and 30 cm diameter, prominently swollen at the base, tapering gradually towards the top, and often bent by the wind. It is smooth with vertical cracks and ringed with prominent irregular leaf scars. Roots are often visible, radiating from the base of the trunk.

Leaves Up to 7 m long with a gently twisted midrib and a long stalk about one quarter of the leaf length. They are pinnately divided into numerous long, pointed, leathery, drooping, glossy, dark-green leaflets, closely and evenly spaced and emerging in a horizontal plane on either side of the midrib. The leaflets are 4-5 cm wide at the base, and up to 1.3 m long with a prominent yellowish central vein and small hairs below. The margins are folded downwards on either side of the central vein. The leaf stalks are green to yellow, flat to deeply concave above and convex below, with a bulbous, fibrous base that partially sheaths the top of the trunk.

Inflorescence A large, dense, much-branched panicle, 1-2 m long, with a stout stalk arising from the leaf axils within the crown, and 20-60 flower-bearing branchlets. It is initially enclosed in 2 pointed, persistent bracts that split open over a 24 hour period allowing the inflorescence to emerge and unfold. A number of inflorescences are often present at the same time, and are produced all year round.

Flowers Cream, to 3 cm across, stalkless, the females are larger than the males and resemble a small coconut, being enclosed in small, scaly bracts. Both sexes are produced on the same inflorescence, the females at the bases of the branchlets and the males clustered at the ends. Both have 3 sepals and 3 petals; the males have 6 stamens and a rudimentary pistil; the females a 3-celled ovary, each cell containing one ovule, and 3 stigmas.

Fruits Large, green, yellow or reddish-brown drupes, 20-30 cm long, ovoid with 3 sides separated by ridges. The coconut comprises a fibrous husk, 1-5 cm thick, surrounding the seed, which has a hard, brown, woody shell, 3-6 mm thick, with 3 pores at the base, around a thin, white, oily flesh enclosing a watery fluid. The fruits take about one year to mature and weigh about 1.5 kg; they are present all year round.

Habitat Tropical seashores and alluvial plains among various types of vegetation, requiring access to an underground water supply. The fruits are distributed by coastal currents and germinate readily, usually within 4-5 months. They require sandy, well-drained soil and lots of water.

Distribution Found along the tropical coast of northern Australia in the NT and Qld, and some of the adjacent islands. They were probably introduced by the early European settlers, but are now naturalised and widely cultivated. They will grow as far south as Sydney in frost free areas.

Family Arecaceae.

Howea belmoreana

Curly or Sentry Palm

Endemic to the mountain slopes of Lord Howe Island and extensively cultivated in temperate Australia, this graceful palm a medium-sized, slender, single-stemmed, feather-leaved palm without a crownshaft. It has a medium-density crown of strongly-arching fronds with erect, upward-pointing leaflets, and distinctive long, pendulous, unbranched fruiting spikes.

Trunk Brownish-green to grey in older specimens, 5-12 m tall and 8-18 cm diameter, but rarely exceeding 5 m in cultivation, except in crowded conditions. It is smooth and ringed with prominent, closely-spaced, pale, horizontal leaf scars, and is usually enlarged at the base.

Leaves Up to 5 m long with a slender, arching midrib and a smooth, green, slender stalk, 1-2 m long. They are pinnately divided into numerous closely and evenly spaced leaflets, dull-green on both surfaces, forward-pointing and attached at an upward angle to the midrib of the frond to form a V-shape. The leaflets are 30-60 cm long and 2-3 cm wide, fairly stiff, lanceolate with long, pointed tips, a prominent raised central vein and 2 side veins visible on the upper surface. The terminal leaflets are separate and divided to their bases. The leaf stalks are convex below and concave above with a raised central ridge and a bulbous, partially sheathing base with brownish-grey fibrous margins.

Inflorescence A slender, unbranched, erect, becoming pendulous spike to about 2 m long with a slightly flattened stalk about 50 cm long. Several inflorescences are usually present at the same time. They arise from the bases of the leaves within the crown or from the upper leaf scars, and are initially enclosed in a long, brown, papery, cylindrical bract that falls before the flowers open.

Flowers About 1 cm long; both male and female flowers are produced on the same inflorescence, typically arranged with one female between 2 males in recesses along the flowering spike. Male flowers are creamy-brown with 3 overlapping sepals and 3 larger woody petals, their edges touching in bud, with 30-40 short stamens and a small sterile pistil. Female flowers are green with 3 overlapping sepals and petals and a single-celled ovary with a 3-lobed stigma; they mature after the male flowers.

Fruits Smooth, shiny-green, turning reddish-brown when ripe. They are hard and ovoid, 25-40 mm long and 2-3 cm diameter with a slightly extended, flattened tip. They comprise a single ovate seed about 15 mm long, with looping strands of fibres on the surface, surrounded by a thin, dry, fibrous coat and a slightly fleshy outer layer.

Habitat Naturally occurring in large colonies or as a forest understorey on steep mountain slopes in coral sands or volcanic soils, from sea level to about 450 m, in a temperate climate. The fresh seed germinates within 2-12 months, preferring light, sandy soil with partial shade and moist conditions. The mature palms will tolerate full sun and light frosts.

Distribution Endemic to Lord Howe Island, but commonly cultivated in parks and gardens in temperate areas of Australia as far south as Melbourne.

Family Arecaceae.

Howea forsteriana   **Kentia or Thatch Palm**

The Kentia Palm is a medium-sized, slender, single-stemmed, feather-leaved palm endemic to coastal areas of Lord Howe Island, but extensively cultivated in temperate Australia. A graceful palm lacking a crownshaft, it has a wide, spreading crown of stiff, slightly arching fronds with drooping leaflets and a clustered inflorescence of long, unbranched flowering spikes.

Trunk Green turning brownish-grey, 5-15 m tall and 8-16 cm diameter, often with a slightly swollen base, and rarely exceeding 5 m in uncrowded open sites. It is smooth and ringed with irregular horizontal and oblique leaf scars, well-spaced towards the top of the trunk and closely-spaced at the base.

Leaves Up to 5 m long with a long, slender, straight or slightly curved stalk, 1-1.5 m long, flattened to slightly ridged above, convex, dark-green with whitish scurf below. The leaves are pinnately divided into numerous closely and evenly spaced, opposite, distinctly drooping leaflets, dull dark-green on both surfaces with small brown scales below, attached to the upper surface of the midrib on either side of the central ridge. The leaflets are 30-100 cm long and 2-4 cm wide, lanceolate with long, pointed tips, a constricted base with the margins folded down. They have a prominent yellowish central vein raised on the upper surface, and a number of parallel veins giving the leaflets a slightly corrugated appearance. The broad base of the leaf stalk has brown fibrous margins and encircles the top of the trunk with masses of fibre.

Inflorescence About 1 m long with 3-7 dark-green to brown, slender, pendulous spikes attached at their bases to a short, common, flattened stalk. Several inflorescences are usually present at the same time, arising from the bases of the lower leaves within the crown or from the upper leaf scars. Each spike is initially enclosed in a long, grey, papery, cylindrical bract which is shed before the flowers open.

Flowers About 1 cm long, both male and female flowers are produced on the same inflorescence, typically arranged with one female between 2 males in recesses along the flowering spikes. Male flowers are creamy-brown with 3 overlapping sepals and 3 larger woody petals, their edges touching in bud, with 80-100 short stamens and a small sterile pistil. Female flowers are green with 3 overlapping sepals and petals, and a single-celled ovary with a 3-lobed stigma; they mature after the male flowers.

Fruits Smooth, shiny-green turning dull-orange or red when ripe. They are hard and ovoid, 3-5 cm long and 2 cm diameter with a slightly pointed tip. The fruits comprise a single large seed about 2 cm long, with looping strands of fibres on the surface, surrounded by a thin, dry, fibrous coat and a slightly fleshy outer layer. They are closely packed on the stalk.

Habitat Naturally occurring in pure stands on low coastal temperate areas in coral sands or basaltic soils, to 300 m altitude. The fresh seed usually germinates within 2 months. The plants prefer rich, well-drained soil with plenty of water and partial shade when young. The mature palms will tolerate full sun and light frosts.

Distribution Endemic to Lord Howe Island, but commonly cultivated in parks and gardens in temperate parts of Australia as far south as Melbourne.

Family Arecaceae.

Laccospadix australasica
Atherton Palm

The Atherton Palm is a small, slender, single-stemmed or clumping, feather-leaved palm of the mountain areas of northeastern Queensland. This is an elegant understorey rainforest species usually with a number of slender trunks without crownshafts. The fronds arise from the upper part of the trunk on erect, slender stalks that arch as the leaves age to form a graceful, dark-green, spreading crown with upright fronds in the centre. The fruits form distinctive, closely-packed, long, red, pendulous clusters.

Stems Dark-green turning yellowish-brown to grey, 2-8 m tall and 5-15 cm diameter. They are covered with fibrous leaf bases, becoming smooth and prominently ringed with closely-spaced brown leaf scars.

Leaves Up to 2.5 m long with slender stalks to 1.3 m long. They are pinnately divided into 18-24 pairs of evenly-spaced leaflets, dull dark-green above and slightly paler below, arising at a slight upward angle to the midrib, and drooping slightly towards the tips. The leaflets are 30-70 cm long and 2-4 cm wide, linear to lanceolate with narrow, pointed tips. They have 3-5 prominent parallel main veins, raised on the upper surface. New leaves are an attractive deep-reddish colour. The leaf stalks are mid-green with a few small brown scales on the lower surface. They are convex below and slightly ridged above, with sharp margins and a fibrous base that partially encircles the top of the trunk.

Inflorescence An unbranched, semi-pendulous spike, 0.5-1.6 m long, with a slender, arching stalk 30-60 cm long. Several inflorescences are produced at the same time, arising from the lower leaf bases. They are initially enclosed in a pair of slender, brownish, papery bracts that fall before the flowers open.

Flowers Yellowish-green and about 5 mm across. Both male and female flowers are produced on the same inflorescence. They are typically arranged in groups of 3 with one female between 2 males. The male flowers are slightly larger and mature before the females. Both sexes have 3 sepals and 3 petals, the latter just touching in the males and overlapping in the females. Male flowers have 6-12 stamens and a small sterile pistil. Females have a single-celled ovary containing one ovule.

Fruits Green, turning yellow to scarlet or bright shiny-red when ripe. They are 10-15 mm long, ovoid with a black, pointed tip, and densely packed on the stalk to form a long, attractive, necklace-like, pendulous, fruiting spike. The fruits comprise a large seed with a fibrous coat surrounded by a thin, fleshy, outer layer.

Habitat Naturally occurring in scattered to dense colonies in rainforests at elevations of 500-1600m, in high rainfall areas with cool nights. This is an understorey palm, growing beneath the canopy in full shade. Fresh seed germinates easily within 3-5 months. The young plants prefer rich, loamy soil in shady sites, and will tolerate slight frosts. They can also be propagated by division of the suckers.

Distribution Endemic to the mountains and tablelands of northeastern Qld, from Innisfail to Mt Amos, where they are locally common.

Family Arecaceae.

Linospadix microcarya

This delicate palm is a small, slender, clumping, feather-leaved palm growing as an understorey species in the rainforests of northeastern Australia. It has 1-3 dominant stems and a number of suckers around the base which grow when the main stem dies. It lacks a crownshaft, and has a compact or extended crown of small arching fronds each bearing 6-12 pairs of leaflets.

Stem Dark-green to greyish-brown, very slender, to 2 m tall and 5-10 mm diameter. It is straight, smooth and ringed with prominent, closely-spaced, horizontal leaf scars.

Leaves Up to 60 cm long with a thin midrib and very short, smooth, slender, arching, stalk with a broad, bulbous, sheathing base that encircles the top of the stem. The leaves are pinnately divided into 12-24 thin, alternate, regularly spaced, forward-pointing leaflets, mid to dark-green on both surfaces. The leaflets are linear to lanceolate, 10-25 cm long and 1-2 cm wide with pointed or shallowly-toothed tips, and a prominent midvein raised on the upper surface. The terminal pair are united at their bases to form a fish-tail shape. Occasionally the lowermost pairs and some of the intermediate leaflets are united at their bases.

Inflorescence A slender, unbranched, semi-erect, becoming pendulous, spike, 45-85 cm long, with a slender green stalk. Several inflorescences are usually present at the same time, arising from the axils of the older leaves within the crown. They are initially enclosed in 2 papery brown bracts, the lower bract is short and hidden among the leaf bases, the upper bract is much longer, wrapped around the inflorescence, and splits open along one side before the flowers open.

Flowers About 2 mm across, both male and female flowers are produced on the same inflorescence. Male flowers are creamy-yellow with 3 sepals and 3 fleshy narrow ovate petals and 6-15 stamens. They mature and are shed before the females open. Female flowers are yellow-orange, globular, with a small opening. They have 3 sepals and petals, a single-celled ovary containing one ovule, and 3 tiny stigmas. The flowers are spirally arranged around the inflorescence, typically in groups of 3 with one female between 2 males.

Fruits Creamy-yellow or orange-red when ripe. They are spherical with a small pointed tip, 5-8 mm long, and have a single seed surrounded by a thin layer of edible flesh. They are arranged around the pendulous stalk of the inflorescence to form a long, necklace-like fruiting spike.

Habitat Naturally occurring in lowland and intermediate tropical rainforests where they are scattered understorey plants. The fresh seed germinates readily in 4-6 months, and the plants can be grown from suckers around the base. They are slow growing and prefer rich, well-drained soil and plenty of water in shaded, protected, frost-free sites.

Distribution Scattered in northeastern Qld from sea-level to about 1100 m altitude.

Family Arecaceae.

Linospadix minor

This delicate palm is a small, slender, single-stemmed or clumping, feather-leaved palm growing as an understorey species in the rainforests of northeastern Australia and New Guinea. It often has 1-2 dominant stems and a number of suckers around the base which grow when the main stem dies. It lacks a crownshaft, and has a sparse crown of small arching fronds each bearing only 6-8 pairs of leaflets.

Stem Green to brownish-green, very slender, to 1.6 m tall and 6-20 mm wide. The stem is straight, smooth and ringed with closely-spaced, horizontal leaf scars.

Leaves From 60-100 cm long with a thin midrib and a smooth, slender, arching, pale-green stalk 10-20 cm long. The leaves are pinnately divided into 12-16 thin, alternate, regularly spaced, slightly upward-pointing, dull green leaflets. The leaflets are 15-35 cm long and 2-5 cm wide, narrowed at the base, with oblique, irregularly-toothed, jagged tips, a prominent midvein and 2 prominent longitudinal veins raised on the upper surface. The terminal pair are united at their bases to form a fish-tail shape. The leaf stalk is slightly flattened above and convex below, with a broad, ribbed, bulbous sheathing base that almost surrounds the top of the stem.

Inflorescence A slender, unbranched, erect, becoming pendulous, spike, 40-90 cm long, with a slender stalk about 4 mm wide. Several inflorescences are usually present at the same time, arising from the axils of the lower leaves. They are initially enclosed in 2 papery brown, bracts, the lower bract is short and hidden among the leaf bases, the upper bract is much longer, wraps around the inflorescence, and splits open along one side before the flowers open.

Flowers Green to yellow, very small, both male and female flowers are produced on the same inflorescence. Male flowers are creamy-yellow, about 5 mm across when fully open, with 3 sepals, 3 fleshy narrow ovate petals and 6-15 stamens. They mature and are shed before the females open. Female flowers are green with 3 sepals and petals, a single-celled ovary containing one ovule, and 3 tiny stigmas. The flowers are spirally arranged around the inflorescence, typically in groups of 3 with one female between 2 males.

Fruits Yellow or pink to red when ripe. They are narrow ovoid, 12-18 mm long, with a single seed surrounded by a thin layer of edible flesh. The fruits are crowded along the pendulous stalk of the inflorescence, forming a necklace-like fruiting spike.

Habitat Naturally occurring in shady sites in tropical and subtropical rainforests where they are scattered understorey plants. The fresh seed germinates readily in 4-6 months, and the plants can be grown from suckers around the base. They are very slow-growing and prefer rich, well-drained soil and plenty of water in shaded, protected, frost-free sites.

Distribution Common and widespread in northeastern Qld and extending into New Guinea. They are easily grown and cultivated in parks and gardens as far south as Sydney.

Family Arecaceae.

Linospadix monostachya   **Walking Stick Palm**

The Walking Stick Palm is a small, very slender, single-stemmed, feather-leaved palm growing as an understorey species in the subtropical rainforests of the east coast of Australia. This delicate palm has attractive strings of red fruits, it lacks a crownshaft, and has a fairly dense, spreading crown with many short, dark-green fronds with irregularly shaped leaflets.

Stem Green turning dark-brown, very slender, to about 5 m tall, but usually 1-3.5 m tall and 2-3 cm diameter. It is straight with a slightly swollen base, smooth, woody, ringed with greyish-brown, closely-spaced horizontal leaf scars, and sometimes with visible roots.

Leaves From 30-130 cm long with a thin midrib and a smooth, slender, arching stalk, 12-30 cm long,. The leaves are pinnately divided into a variable number of both broad and narrow leaflets, dull to glossy dark-green on both surfaces, forward-pointing and very irregularly spaced along the midrib. The leaflets are 20-30 cm long and variable in width, they taper to oblique, pointed tips, some are fused at their bases and have a number of distinct teeth at their tips. The terminal pair are united at their bases to form a fish-tail shape. The leaf stalk is flattish above and convex below with a few brown scales, and a broad, bulbous base partially sheathing the stem.

Inflorescence A slender, unbranched, semi-pendulous, becoming pendulous, spike, 1-1.5 m long with a slender green stalk about 40 cm long. Several inflorescences are usually present at the same time. They arise from the lower leaf bases and are initially enclosed in 2 thin brown papery bracts, the lower bract is short and hidden among the leaf bases, the upper bract is much longer, wraps around the inflorescence and falls before the flowers open.

Flowers Small, green to cream. Both male and female flowers are produced on the same inflorescence. Male flowers are ovate, 6-8 mm long and 4 mm wide, creamy-yellow with 3 small overlapping sepals and 3 larger egg-shaped to oblong, pointed, stiff, hard lobes with their edges touching in bud, and opening only sightly. They have 8-12 yellow stamens and fall before the female flowers open. Female flowers are 8-12 mm long, greenish-yellow with 3 overlapping sepals and petals, a single-celled ovary containing one ovule, and 3 tiny stigmas. The flowers are spirally arranged along the inflorescence, typically in groups of 3 with one female between 2 males. Flowering occurs throughout the year.

Fruits Waxy, yellow-orange to bright-red when ripe. The fruits are ovoid to elliptical, 10-15 mm across, with a thin, edible, acidic, fleshy layer surrounding a single seed. They are crowded into a colourful, pendulous, necklace-like spike.

Habitat Naturally occurring in subtropical rainforests, and occasionally in cool-temperate rainforests, often along stream banks, in shady sites, where they may grow in scattered colonies. The fresh seed germinates readily in 4-6 months, preferring complete shade, lots of water, good drainage and rich soil. They are slow-growing and will tolerate cold climates and mild frost.

Distribution Common from around Gympie in southeastern Qld to the Singleton district on the southern north coast of NSW, growing mainly in highland sites at the northern extent of their range.

Family Arecaceae.

MW.

Linospadix palmeriana

This delicate palm is a small, slender, clumping, feather-leaved palm growing as an understorey species in the highland rainforests of northeastern Australia. It has 1-3 dominant stems and a number of suckers around the base that grow when the main stem dies. It has a compact or extended crown of 6-10 small arching fronds, each bearing 2-4 pairs of leaflets.

Stem Dark-green to greyish-brown, very slender, to 2 m tall and 5-10 mm diameter. It is straight, smooth, woody and ringed with prominent, relatively widely-spaced horizontal leaf scars.

Leaves Are 20-45 cm long with a thin midrib and very short, smooth, slender and arching stalk with a broad, bulbous, sheathing base that encircles the top of the stem. The leaves are pinnately divided into 4-8 thin, stiff, opposite, regularly spaced, forward-pointing leaflets, dark-green above and slightly paler below. The leaflets are very shallowly S-shaped with a broad base and gently curving margins forming a long point. They are 15-30 cm long and 2-5 cm wide with 4-5 prominent raised midveins on the upper surface. The terminal pair form a fish-tail shape with slightly toothed tips. Broad and narrow leaflets may both be present on the same leaf; the narrow ones occupy the middle portion of the leaf.

Inflorescence A slender, unbranched, semi-erect, becoming pendulous, spike, 15-45 cm long, with a slender stalk. Several inflorescences are usually present at the same time, arising from the axils of the upper leaves within the crown. They are initially enclosed in 2 papery, brown bracts, the lower one short and hidden among the leaf bases, the upper one is much longer, wraps around the inflorescence, and splits open along one side before the flowers open.

Flowers About 4 mm across; both male and female flowers are produced on the same inflorescence. They are spirally arranged around the inflorescence, typically in groups of 3 with one female between 2 males. Male flowers have 3 sepals, 3 fleshy, narrow-ovate petals, and 6-15 stamens. They mature and are shed before the female flowers open. Female flowers have 3 sepals and 3 petals, a single-celled ovary containing one ovule, and 3 tiny stigmas.

Fruits Yellowish-orange or red when ripe, cylindrical to ovoid, 8-10 mm long with a small pointed tip and a single seed surrounded by a thin, fleshy layer. They are arranged around the pendulous stalk of the inflorescence to form a long, necklace-like fruiting spike.

Habitat Naturally occurring in highland tropical rainforests where they are scattered understorey plants in very shady sites. Fresh seed germinates readily in 4-6 months, and plants can be grown from suckers around the base. They prefer rich, well-drained soil and plenty of water in cool, shaded, protected, frost-free sites.

Distribution Scattered in northeastern Qld above 800m, particularly in the Bellenden Ker Range.

Family Arecaceae.

Nypa fruticans
Nypa or Mangrove Palm

The Nypa Palm is a large, stout, clumping, feather-leaved palm to 10 m tall, growing along estuaries in northern Australia and tropical Asia. This unusual palm has 4-7 large, erect, arching fronds arising from a thick underground stem, and bears pandan-like fruit.

Stems Are 30-50 cm diameter and branch dichotomously to form large clumps. They are buried in soft mud.

Leaves Are 5-10 m long, including the smooth, stout, cylindrical leaf stalks which are 1-1.6 m long and about 45 mm across at the bottom leaflet. The leaves are stiff and pinnately divided into 80-120 alternate, regularly-spaced, drooping leaflets, shiny-green with a whitish bloom above, dull and paler below. The leaflets are lanceolate, 60-180 cm long and 5-9 cm wide, smaller at the base and at the tip of the frond, with long, finely-pointed tips, thickened marginal veins and prominent yellow midveins raised on the upper surface. The leaflets are forward-pointing with constricted bases and curled-under margins. They arise from the upper surface of the pale-green, scurfy midrib on either side of a narrow central ridge. The leaf stalks are green to reddish-brown with grey or brownish bases that expand to partially sheath the top of the stem.

Inflorescence A stout, erect panicle with a thick stalk, 0.75-2.4 m long, terminating in a globular head of female flowers, 20-25 cm across, with several ascending lateral branches bearing short, dense spikes of male flowers. The inflorescence arises from the base of the leaves in the centre of the crown. It is sheathed by 3 large, leathery, orange tipped with olive green, strap-like bracts and many smaller sheathing bracts. After shedding their pollen the male flowers and their branches quickly shrivel up, leaving a terminal cluster of fruits developing from the female flowers.

Flowers Either male or female and produced on the same inflorescence. Male flowers are 4-6 mm long, cream, with 3 oblong, pointed sepals, 3 similar petals and 3 stamens united into a central protruding column. They are tightly packed to form cylindrical spikes 4-6 cm long and surrounded at the base by bracts. Female flowers are lemon-yellow, about 1 cm long with 6 pointed tepals about 4 mm long, and 3 woody, angular carpels about 1 cm long, each containing a single ovule. They are closely packed into a terminal, globular head about 4 cm across, partially enclosed by bracts.

Fruits Shiny chestnut-brown to black when ripe, joined in a globular, terminal, somewhat pineapple-like fruiting body, 30-50 cm diameter. This comprises many closely-packed, 2-4 angled segments, each about 9-15 cm long and 5-10 cm across, with narrow fibrous bases and rounded pyramidal tips topped by the pointed remains of the stigmas. The fruits are smooth with a fleshy, fibrous layer surrounding a single, grooved, kidney-shaped seed about 45 mm across. The fruits float and are distributed by ocean currents.

Habitat Grows in slightly saline water in tropical coastal regions along muddy tidal river banks, forming extensive colonies, fringing steeply-shelving banks or covering large, low-lying areas.

Distribution Scattered in colonies on the Cobourg Peninsula and Melville Island in the NT, along the northeastern coast of Qld as far south as Halifax Bay, extending into tropical Asian islands and coastal regions of the Indian Ocean.

Family Arecaceae.

Oraniopsis appendiculata

This robust palm is a medium-sized, single-stemmed, feather-leaved palm of the dense tropical rain-forests of northeastern Australia. It lacks a crownshaft and has a light to medium density spreading crown of 8-15 dark-green, stiff fronds with pale undersurfaces.

Trunk Grey to dark-brown, usually growing to about 6 m tall and 20 cm diameter, although some specimens are 20 m tall and 45 cm diameter. The trunk is smooth, dotted with small pores, hard and woody near the base (which is slightly swollen), soft and fibrous near the top, and ringed with closely-spaced, horizontal leaf scars.

Leaves Up to 6 m long with stout leaf stalks, 80-100 cm long and 7-8 cm across at the base. The leaves are pinnately divided into 100-220 opposite, forward-pointing, well-spaced leaflets, glossy dark-green above and densely covered with short, felt-like, light-grey to yellowish hairs below. The leaflets are up to 1 m long and 5 cm across, linear to narrow-lanceolate with narrow, oblique, pointed tips. They are stiff and leathery with a prominent yellow midvein raised on the upper surface that ends before the tip of the leaflet, and 2 green lines alongside it on the lower surface. The terminal leaflets are united at their bases and have cleft tips. New growth is reddish. The leaf stalks are pale-green turning black with age. They have smooth sharp margins and are sometimes covered with soft brown matted hairs on the underside. They are convex below and have a deeply-concave upper surface near the base; the midribs are flattened and ridged above. The leaf bases are very bulbous and partially sheath the trunk with brown fibres.

Inflorescence A much-branched, drooping panicle, 75-120 cm long and covered with short, brown, matted hair. A number of inflorescences may be present at the same time, arising from the leaf bases within the crown, on short, thick, flattened stalks. They are initially enclosed in 3-5 large bracts. The largest bract is 60-135 cm long with a pointed tip, and splits down one side to release the flowering branches before being shed.

Flowers White to cream and about 8 mm across. Male and female flowers are produced on the same inflorescence. They are closely packed on the branches, singly, in pairs or groups of 3 with one female between 2 males. They both have 3 free, fleshy, narrowly-triangular petals and 3 tiny sepals forming a cup. Male flowers have 6 fleshy stamens and a very small, sterile pistil. Females have a 3-celled ovary, each with one ovule, 3 spreading stigmas and 6 sterile stamens; 1-2 ovules may develop into seeds.

Fruits Produced in a dense cluster. They are green turning yellow, spherical, 35-40 mm diameter, with short stalks, pointed tips and 1-2 small appendages near the base. They usually contain one large spherical and poisonous seed surrounded by a white pulpy layer with a smooth outer skin, although 2 seeds may develop in separate lobes.

Habitat Dense tropical rainforests along creek beds or hillsides, in shady sites in moist, deep, rich soils. They are very slow growing and cold tolerant, developing a trunk after 20-30 years. The fresh seed germinates slowly and sporadically over several years.

Distribution Confined to the coast and tablelands of northeastern Qld from Innisfail to just south of Cooktown, from 300 m to 1500 m altitude.

Family Arecaceae.

Phoenix canariensis   **Canary Island Date Palm**

The Canary Island Date Palm is a tall, stout, single-stemmed, feather-leaved palm native to the Canary Islands, but widely cultivated and naturalised in parts of Australia. This familiar species has a luxuriant, spreading crown of up to 200 densely-packed, arching and often slightly twisted fronds atop a distinctive, thick trunk which lacks a crownshaft. A number of dead fronds usually hang from the top of the trunk.

Trunk Brown to greyish-brown, stout and thick, to 20 m high and 1.3 m diameter. It is very woody, and retains the persistent leaf bases in younger specimens. These are eventually shed to leave a diamond pattern of leaf scars in older palms. The trunk is straight, often bulges at the base, and may support a number of epiphytic plants.

Leaves Up to 6 m long, arching and strongly ascending with a very short, stout leaf stalk. The leaves are pinnately divided into 300-400 closely-spaced, forward and upward pointing, linear to lanceolate leaflets. The leaflets are dull green on both surfaces, thick but not rigid, and the lower ones are reduced to flat spines. Leaflets are 15-55 cm long and 15-40 mm wide, folded upwards at the base, with a prominent, channelled, yellow midvein raised on the lower surface, and thickened marginal veins. They are clustered in groups of 2-3 near the base of the leaf, turned in various directions to the midrib towards the centre, and equidistant and more or less opposite in the upper half of the leaf. The leaf stalks are pale-green, sometimes with brown or whitish scales, convex below and flat above with a wide, flattened base with dark-brown fibrous margins.

Inflorescence A densely-branched, semi-erect panicle, shorter than the leaves, about 2 m long with a long, flattened, stout, pale-green to yellow stalk. A number of inflorescences are usually pre-sent at the same time, arising from the leaf bases among the crown.

Flowers Are borne on separate male and female plants. Male flowers are creamy-yellow, about 12 mm long, ovate, with 3 sepals and 3 thin, striped, leathery, pointed petals. They are alternate, often in pairs. Female flowers are pale-orange, about 7 mm long, globular, with 3 sepals and 3 petals. They are massed on the inflorescence.

Fruits Green becoming orange when ripe, ovate to globular with a small pointed tip, about 2 cm long and 1 cm diameter, containing a single, grooved, ovate-elliptic seed surrounded by a fleshy outer layer.

Habitat Naturally occurring in coastal areas in full sun. They are very hardy and will tolerate frost, heat and poor soils in coastal and inland sites, although they require well drained soil. The fresh seed germinates readily in 1-2 months.

Distribution Endemic to the Canary islands, although they are cultivated throughout the warmer parts of the world. They are naturalised in parts of Australia, and are common in parks and gardens from the tropics to temperate areas.

Family Arecaceae.

Phoenix dactylifera **Date Palm**

A tall, fairly slender, single-stemmed or clumping feather-leaved palm native to North Africa, but widely cultivated throughout the world, and naturalised in parts of Australia, where it is a familiar sight. This species lacks a crownshaft and has a fairly loose, spreading crown of 20-40 or more fronds. The base of the trunk in younger specimens is usually surrounded by a mass of suckers, some of which may develop into mature trees.

Trunk Brown to greyish-brown, to 40 m high and 30-40 cm diameter. It is very woody and younger specimens retain the persistent leaf bases. Older plants have a diamond-shaped pattern of closely packed leaf scars. The trunk often bulges at the base where suckers are produced, and may support a number of epiphytic plants.

Leaves Up to 7 m long, arching and strongly ascending with a long, slender, flattened, spiny leaf stalk, with long, slender, sharp spines along the margins replacing the lowest leaflets. The leaves are pinnately divided into numerous crowded and evenly spaced stiff, rigid, forward-pointing leaflets, dull greyish-green on both surfaces. They are in groups of 2-3 on either side of the upper surface of the midrib, attached in the same plane or at various angles. The leaf stalks are pale-green to grey, about 4-6 cm across, flat and ridged above and convex below with a slight ridge, becoming flatter towards the fibrous base. The leaflets are 20-65 cm long and 15-20 mm wide, narrow linear with a long, sharp point. They have a prominent central vein, raised below, numerous parallel veins and a constricted base with the margins folded upwards.

Inflorescence A densely-branched panicle, about 1.2 m long, shorter than the leaves, with a pale-green to yellow flattened stalk and a sheathing bract that encloses the inflorescence in bud before falling away. A number of inflorescences are usually present at the same time, they arise from the leaf bases among the crown, and are erect, becoming pendulous in fruit, on stout, rigid stalks.

Flowers Borne on separate male and females plants. The males are creamy-white, 5-10 mm long with 3 sepals united into a small cup, 3 pointed leathery petals with their edges touching in bud, usually with 6 stamens. The females are yellow with 3 sepals united into a 3-lobed cup, 3 overlapping petals and 6 united, scale-like stamens.

Fruits Green becoming deep orange or yellowish-brown when ripe, oblong to ovoid, 5-7 cm long and 2-3 cm diameter, containing a single, grooved, cylindrical seed surrounded by a thick, fleshy, edible and very sweet outer layer. The plants bear annually for well over 100 years, requiring hot, dry conditions to produce sweet, edible fruits, and may carry over 50 kg of dates.

Habitat They thrive luxuriantly in dry hot areas with access to ground water. They are very hardy, sun-loving, and will tolerate frost, heat and poor well-drained soils in coastal and inland sites. The fresh seed germinates slowly, and may take 4-5 months. The suckers transplant easily.

Distribution Their origin is obscure, although thought to be North Africa. They are widespread throughout the hot, dry parts of the world and extensively cultivated for their dates and ornamental value. In parts of Australia they have become naturalised and are cultivated in tropical, subtropical and temperate areas as far south as Melbourne.

Family Arecaceae.

Calamus australis

Lawyer Cane is a tall, slender, clumping, feather-leaved climbing palm of the lowland and highland rainforests of northeastern Australia. This common species forms impenetrable thickets in rainforest margins and clearings, with many stems arising from an underground rhizome. The sheathed stems are armed with sharp reddish-brown spines up to 8 cm long, usually joined into groups, while the leaf stalks and midribs bear scattered spines. Slender, flexible climbing structures, known as flagella, arise from the top of the leaf sheaths opposite the leaf stalks. These are 2-3 m long and armed with numerous recurved hooks that attach themselves to other vegetation and cling tenaciously to clothing. They have no crown, the leaves being fairly closely-spaced along the upper half of the stems.

Stems Green turning yellow with age, long, slender and flexible, 2-3 cm diameter and sheathed by the spiny leaf bases.

Leaves Up to 2.5 m long with short stalks 4-5 cm long. The leaf stalks are flattened and covered with spines above, convex and armed with small claws below. They have a sheathing base that surrounds the stem and is densely covered with very long, reddish-brown spines up to 8 cm long. The leaves are pinnately divided into 20-36 narrow-lanceolate, pale to dark shiny-green leaflets, unevenly spaced and arising in a horizontal plane on each side of the arching midrib, which bears a few hooks. The leaflets are 10-30 cm long and 2-3 cm wide, narrowly constricted with curved-down margins at their bases. They have a prominent raised central vein and 2 or more noticeable parallel veins. The margins are armed with a few small spines.

Inflorescence A long, slender, pendulous, sparsely-branched panicle, 2-3 m long, terminating in a slender, clawed flagellum. The main stem and branches are armed with black-tipped hooks. Each branch has a tubular bract at the base which persists when the flowers open. The branches are divided into a number of small flower-bearing branchlets. Several inflorescences are usually present at the same time, arising from the top of the leaf sheaths of the upper leaves opposite the leaf stalks.

Flowers Creamy-green and ovate. Male and female flowers are borne on separate plants. Male flowers are very small, about 2 mm long, and usually occur singly along the branchlets of the inflorescence. Females are 3-4 mm long and occur in pairs. Both have 3 sepals and 3 petals, 6 stamens and a pistil. In the males the pistil is sterile and in the females the sterile stamens form a ring. The female ovary has 3 cells each containing one ovule, a short style and 3-lobed stigma.

Fruits Cream to white when ripe, globular with a small point at one end, 8-14 mm across and covered with small overlapping scales. They have a single ovoid seed surrounded by a thin, edible, fleshy outer layer.

Habitat Naturally occurring in lowland and highland rainforests, forming prickly impenetrable thickets along the forest margins and in clearings. Fresh seed germinates readily within 4 months. Seedlings are difficult to transplant and prefer a cool, shady site and rich, well-drained soil. They are hardy and will grow in temperate areas.

Distribution Common in northeastern Qld from sea level to above 1000 m on the Atherton Tablelands. They are rarely cultivated due to their thorns and prickles, although they will grow as far south as Sydney.

Family Arecaceae.

Calamus caryotoides
Fish-tail Lawyer Cane

A tall, slender, clumping, feather-leaved climbing palm of the tropical rainforests of northeastern Australia, this palm often forms a tangled thicket with a number of stems. They have needle-like spines on the leaf sheaths and scattered spines on the leaves. Slender, whip-like, flexible climbing structures, known as flagella, arise from the top of the leaf sheaths opposite the stalks. These are 1-2.5 m long and armed with numerous recurved hooks that attach themselves to other vegetation and cling tenaciously to clothing. They have no crown, the leaves being distributed along the stems at fairly wide intervals. The leaflets are wedge-shaped and the terminal pair united to form a fish-tail shape.

Stem Green turning brown with age, slender and wiry, exceeding 5-10 m in length and 7-10 mm across. The stem is hard and shiny where the spiny leaf sheaths have fallen away, and climbs up nearby trees to reach the top of the canopy.

Leaves Are 20-70 cm long, stalkless with a sheathing base that surrounds the stem and is covered with straight brown spines. The leaves are pinnately divided into 6-12 wedge-shaped, alternate, shiny, pale-green leaflets, widely and evenly spaced in a horizontal plane on each side of the midrib. The leaflets are 10-20 cm long and 4-6 cm wide with finely toothed or jagged broad tips and constricted bases with turned-down margins. The terminal pair are fused at their bases to form a fish-tail shape. The midrib is well-armed with curved, brown-tipped thorns. The leaflet margins and surfaces bear a few small, scattered, straight spines.

Inflorescence A long pendulous panicle, 1-2.5 m long with a few short branches. Each branch has a short tubular bract which persists when the flowers open and is divided into a number of smaller, flower-bearing branchlets. Several inflorescences are usually present at the same time, arising from the top of the leaf sheaths of the upper leaves opposite the leaf stalks.

Flowers Cream, 3-4 mm across. Male and female flowers are borne on separate plants on the outer or middle branchlets of the inflorescence. The males usually occur singly and the females in pairs. Both have 3 sepals and 3 petals, 6 stamens and a pistil. In the males the pistil is sterile and in the females the sterile stamens form a ring. The female ovary has 3 cells each containing one ovule, a short style and a 3-lobed stigma.

Fruits Cream when ripe, almost spherical, 8-13 mm across and covered with overlapping scales. They have a thin, fleshy, edible outer coat containing a single seed.

Habitat Naturally occurring in drier tropical rainforests and scrubs, along stream banks and breaks in the canopy, often forming prickly impenetrable thickets or climbing to the tree tops to emerge from the surrounding canopy. Fresh seed usually germinates within 6 months. The plants are relatively fast growing and prefer a warm, shady site and rich, well-drained soil. They are very frost-sensitive when young.

Distribution Widely distributed in northeastern Qld from sea level to about 1000m, from Tully to the Iron Range on Cape York Peninsula. They are not commonly cultivated due to their thorns and prickles, although they will grow as far south as Melbourne in protected sites.

Family Arecaceae.

Calamus moti

Yellow Lawyer Cane

Yellow Lawyer Cane is a tall, slender, clumping, feather-leaved climbing palm of the rainforests of northeastern Australia. Clumps of non-climbing or young palms are common understorey plants in undisturbed rainforests, forming impenetrable thickets with many stems arising from an under-ground rhizome, and climbing vigorously when a break in the canopy occurs. They have spiralling rows of long, sharp, yellow spines on the sheathed stems, and recurved thorns on the leaf stalks. Slender, flexible climbing structures, known as flagella, arise from the top of the leaf sheaths oppo-site the stalks. These are 3-4 m long, branching, pendulous, and armed with numerous recurved hooks that attach themselves to other vegetation and to clothing. They have no crown, the leaves being distributed along the stems at fairly wide intervals.

Stem Green turning yellow with age, slender and flexible, exceeding 5-20 m in length and 2-3 cm wide. It is smooth where the spiny leaf sheaths have fallen away, and the numerous stems often wander and loop over trees.

Leaves Up to 4 m long with a very short stalk and a sheathing base that surrounds the stem in a spiral of closely-packed, sharp, bayonet-like spines about 2 cm long. The leaves are pinnately divided into 80-100 linear to lanceolate leaflets, mid-green above and slightly paler below, closely and evenly spaced in a horizontal plane on each side of the midrib. The curving leaf stalk and midrib are armed with scattered clusters of orange-yellow curved thorns. The leaflets are 30-50 cm long and 2-3 cm wide, constricted at their bases with curved-down margins and 3-5 prominent longitudinal veins. Small sharp spines are present on the margins and veins of the upper surface of the leaflets.

Inflorescence A long, slender, pendulous, sparsely-branched panicle terminating in a long, clawed flagellum. Each branch has a short, tubular bract which persists when the flowers open and is divided into a number of smaller, flower-bearing branchlets. Several inflorescences are usually present at the same time, arising from the top of the leaf sheaths of the upper leaves opposite the leaf stalks.

Flowers Cream to white, 3-5 mm across. Male and female flowers are borne on separate plants. Male flowers usually occur singly and the females in pairs. Both have 3 sepals and 3 petals, 6 sta-mens and a pistil. In the males the pistil is sterile and in the females the sterile stamens form a ring. The female ovary has 3 cells each containing one ovule, a short style and 3-lobed stigma.

Fruits Cream when ripe, globular with a small, pointed tip, 8-13 mm across and covered with small overlapping scales. They have a thin fleshy outer coat surrounding a single globular seed.

Habitat Naturally occurring in tropical and subtropical rainforests in high rainfall areas, along stream banks and breaks in the canopy, often forming prickly impenetrable thickets or climbing to the tree tops to emerge from the surrounding canopy. Fresh seed usually germinates within 6-12 months. The plants prefer warm shady sites and rich, well-drained soil. They are frost sensitive when young.

Distribution Common in northeastern Qld from sea level to above 1000 m on the Atherton Tablelands. They are rarely cultivated due to their thorns and prickles, although they will grow as far south as Sydney.

Family Arecaceae.

Calamus muelleri

Wait-a-while

Wait-a-while is a tall, slender, clumping, feather-leaved climbing palm of the subtropical rainforests and moist scrubs of eastern Australia. This palm often forms a tangled thicket with a number of stems arising annually from an underground rhizome. It has spiny leaf sheaths and recurved thorns on the leaf stalks and midribs. Slender flexible climbing structures, known as flagella, arise from the top of the leaf sheaths opposite the stalks. These are 1-2 m long and armed with numerous recurved hooks that attach themselves to other vegetation and passing animals, hence the common name. They have no crown, the leaves being distributed along the stems at fairly wide intervals.

Stem Green turning brown with age, slender and flexible. It is 8-12 mm wide, smooth where the spiny leaf sheaths have fallen away, and often winds up nearby trees, growing to lengths of 180m, making it the longest plant known.

Leaves Up to 100 cm long with a very short stalk and a sheathing base that surrounds the stem and is covered with brown, needle-like spines, about 1 cm long. The leaves are pinnately divided into 9-19 lanceolate leaflets, dark-green on both surfaces, widely and evenly spaced in a horizontal plane on each side of the midrib, with a group of 4 closely-spaced leaflets at the end. The leaflets are 10-20 cm long and 15-60 mm wide. They have needle-like spines on the margins and veins towards the base of the leaflets on both surfaces. The midrib and stalk are armed with curved hooks.

Inflorescence A long, slender, pendulous, flagella-like stalk to about 2 m long, armed with recurved thorns, with a few small, flower-bearing branches towards the end. Each branch has a short tubular bract which persists when the flowers open. Several inflorescences are usually present at the same time, arising from the top of the leaf sheaths of the upper leaves opposite the leaf stalks.

Flowers Cream to greenish, 3-5 mm across. Male and female flowers are borne on separate plants; the males usually occur singly and the females in pairs. Both have 3 sepals and 3 petals, 6 stamens and a pistil. In the males the pistil is sterile and in the females the sterile stamens form a ring. Female flowers have a 3-celled ovary with one ovule in each cell, a short style and a 3-lobed stigma.

Fruits Cream when ripe, globular, 8-15 mm across, covered with overlapping scales. Fruits are hard with a thin, dry, outer coat containing a single seed.

Habitat Naturally occurring in wet subtropical rainforests and scrubs, along stream banks and breaks in the canopy, often forming prickly impenetrable thickets, or climbing to the tree-tops to emerge from the surrounding canopy. Fresh seed usually germinates within 6 months. The plants prefer a warm, shady site and rich, well-drained soil. They will tolerate mild frosts when older.

Distribution Widely distributed in coastal regions from Proserpine in Qld to Bellingen in NSW. They are not commonly cultivated due to their thorns and prickles, although they will grow as far south as Melbourne in protected sites.

Family Arecaceae.

Calamus radicalis

Vicious Hairy Mary

Vicious Hairy Mary is a tall, slender, clumping, feather-leaved climbing palm of the rainforests of northeastern Australia. This extremely prickly species has many stems arising from an underground rhizome, and forms extensive, almost impenetrable thickets in rainforest margins and clearings. It has many sharp brown spines up to 5 cm long on the leaf stalks and sheathed stems, and conspicuous spines on the leaf margins and veins. Slender, flexible, climbing structures, known as flagella, arise from the top of the leaf sheaths opposite the stalks. These are 2-4 m long and armed with numerous recurved hooks that attach themselves to other vegetation and cling tenaciously to clothing. They have no crown, the leaves being crowded along the upper part of the stem.

Stems Green turning yellow with age, long, slender and flexible, 4-5 cm diameter and sheathed by the long, spiny, leaf bases.

Leaves Up to 3 m long, stalkless or with a very short stalk. They are pinnately divided into 80-120 linear to lanceolate leaflets, bright shiny-green on both surfaces. The leaflets are evenly and alternately spaced, to about 3 cm apart, forward-pointing in a horizontal plane on each side of the arching midrib. They have a sheathing base that surrounds the stem and is densely covered with reddish-brown spines up to 5 cm long along the midrib of the leaf. The leaflets are 30-50 cm long and 2-3 cm wide, abruptly narrowed and folded down at the base, with a raised midrib and 2 or more noticeable parallel veins, all bearing widely-spaced, bristly spines. The margins are armed with many short spines.

Inflorescence A long, slender, pendulous, sparsely-branched panicle, 3-4 m long, the main stem and branches are armed with hooks. Each branch has a tubular bract at the base which persists when the flowers open. The branches are divided into a number of small, flower-bearing branchlets. Several inflorescences are usually present at the same time, they arise from the top of the leaf sheaths of the upper leaves opposite the leaf stalks.

Flowers Creamy-green, 3-4 mm across. Male and female flowers are borne on separate plants. Males usually occur singly and the females in pairs. Both have 3 sepals and 3 petals, 6 stamens and a pistil. In the males the pistil is sterile and in the females the sterile stamens form a ring. Female flowers have a 3-celled ovary with one ovule in each cell, a short style and a 3-lobed stigma.

Fruits Cream to white when ripe, globular, with a small point at one end, about 8 mm across and covered with small overlapping scales. They have a single seed surrounded by a thin, fleshy outer layer.

Habitat Naturally occurring in lowland and highland rainforests, forming prickly, impenetrable thickets along rainforest margins and in clearings. Fresh seed germinates readily in 3-4 months. The seedlings are difficult to transplant and prefer a shady site and rich, well-drained soil. They are frost sensitive, but can be grown in protected sites in temperate areas.

Distribution Northeastern Qld, extending from sea level to above 1000 m on the Atherton Tablelands. They are rarely cultivated due to their thorns and prickles.

Family Arecaceae.

Corypha utan (syn *C. elata*) **Gebang Palm**

The Gebang Palm is a tall, single-stemmed, fan-leaved palm of massive proportions, found in the forests and woodlands of the lowland wet tropics of northern Australia and the Indo-Malaysian region. This huge palm lacks a crownshaft and has a large, dense crown of stiff fronds with long, thick, stalks armed with stout spines. This species dies after fruiting, which is preceded by an enormous terminal inflorescence.

Trunk Grey to brownish-grey, to 25 m tall and 1 m diameter. It is covered with persistent leaf bases in younger specimens, which are shed in part as the tree grows, leaving a closely-ringed spiral pattern of leaf scars along the greater part of the trunk.

Leaves Greyish-green to bluish-green, fan-shaped with a distinct midrib. They are 4-6 m long including their thick, stiff, greyish or yellowish stalks. The leaf blades are shorter than the stalks, 2-3 m across, almost orbicular, stiff and thick-textured, partially pleated and divided about half way down into 80-90 broad segments, to 1.6 m long and 8 cm wide, each tapering to a short, forked, pointed tip. The segments curve down on either side of the midrib. The leaf stalks are 2-4 m long and about 8 cm across at the junction with the leaf blade, and wider at the base, which is deeply split where it joins the trunk. They are deeply channelled above and convex below, with black margins bearing closely-spaced, curved, black spines, 1-2 cm long.

Inflorescence A massive terminal panicle, 2-5 m long. It is almost spherical and develops from the top of the trunk, with a thick, central stem and many slightly upward-pointing side branches, dividing twice into smaller, rigid, flower-bearing branchlets, 15-40 cm long. Thousands of branchlets are formed, producing millions of flowers. The palm flowers at about 40-50 years of age, the fronds fall away and the plant expends its energy on the production of flowers and fruit before dying. Flowering has been recorded between August and October.

Flowers White to cream with an unpleasant odour, very small, 3-8 mm across, and borne in dense, elongated clusters of 5-10 flowers, arranged in regular spirals along the branchlets of the inflorescence. They are bisexual, with 3 sepals, 3 petals, 6 stamens and a 3-celled ovary, each cell with one ovule, and a short style with a 3-lobed stigma. Only one ovule develops into a seed.

Fruits Olive-green to brownish, globular with a short stalk, 15-30 mm across. The fruits are edible and have a single, hard-shelled, spherical seed, 12-20 mm diameter, surrounded by a fleshy layer contained in a tough outer skin. Enormous quantities of fruits are produced and take about 18 months to ripen before the tree dies.

Habitat Naturally occurring in large colonies along tidal river and estuarine floodplains on heavy silt and clay soils in tropical monsoonal areas of northern Australia. Fresh seed germinates sporadically in 3-18 months. The seedlings are slow growing and difficult to transplant, and require plenty of water.

Distribution Scattered in the northeast of the NT around the Liverpool and Glyde River mouths, Elcho Island, and the Cape York Peninsula in northern Qld, extending into New Guinea, the Philippines, Indonesia, Malaysia, southern India and Sri Lanka.

Family Arecaceae.

Licuala ramsayi   **Wedge Leaflet Fan Palm**

This striking palm is a tall, slender, single-stemmed, fan-leaved palm of the tropical rainforests of northeastern Australia. It lacks a crownshaft and has a relatively dense crown of large, shiny-green circular leaves with wedge-shaped segments and long, slender, arching stems.

Trunk Grey to dark-brown, to 20 m tall and 20 cm diameter, slightly swollen at the base, sometimes with numerous slender supporting roots extending to 20 cm above the ground. The trunk is fairly smooth and hard with small vertical fissures and often has a collar of fibrous leaf bases. It is faintly ringed with leaf scars, and often covered with patches of lichen.

Leaves Shiny dark-green above and duller below, circular in outline, and divided to the base into many closely-spaced, wedge-shaped segments. The whole, stiff leaf blade is 1-2 m across. The pleated segments radiate from the end of the leaf stalk to a tip 5-8 cm across. They are irregularly notched between the ends of their 4-15 ribs. The slender, arching leaf stalk is dark-green with some brownish scurf on the underside, flat above and convex below, 1.25-2.5 m long, 15-20 mm wide at the tip, and 3-4 cm wide at the base, with a very short outgrowth on the upper surface of the leaf. The leaf stalk is smooth and hard with black spines on the margins of the lower part, and a red-brown, fibrous, sheathing base that splits as the trunk expands, with some of its hessian-like fibres remaining attached to the trunk. The leaf segments of young palms are much more widely spaced than mature specimens. Young leaves are sometimes completely undivided, or the segments may be joined at the apex.

Inflorescence A slender, much-branched, pendulous panicle as long as, or longer than the leaves, and arising from the leaf bases. The main stem is 1.4-2.1 m long, with 7-8 side branches spaced about 15 cm apart, each subtended by a small bract, and further divided into many small, flower-bearing branchlets. The branches are sheathed in persistent smooth, overlapping, tubular bracts that often resemble a crown, with expanded toothed or pointed tips when the fruit matures. A number of inflorescences are usually present at the same time.

Flowers Cream, very small and produced in large clusters. They are bisexual, tubular, with 6 stamens united at their base, and a 3-celled ovary joined at the top into a single style with a small, sometimes 3-lobed stigma.

Fruits Green turning bright-orange or red when ripe, spherical or ovoid, about 1 cm across, comprising a single seed surrounded by a thin, fleshy layer.

Habitat Naturally occurring in low-lying coastal tropical rainforests, along stream banks and swampy sites. They often grow in extensive colonies, establishing themselves under existing canopies. Fresh seed germinates within 6 months in rich, well-drained soil. They are very slow-growing and require warm, shady sites with plenty of water.

Distribution Locally common along the coast of northeastern Qld from the tip of the Cape York Peninsula to near Tully, usually within 20 km of the coast, from sea level to 450 m.

Family Arecaceae.

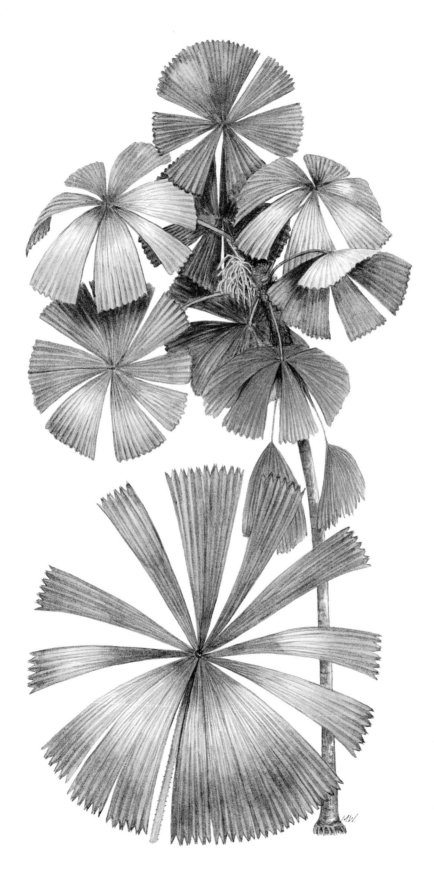

Livistona australis

Cabbage or Fan Palm

The Cabbage Palm is a tall, single-stemmed, fan-leaved palm of the warm temperate to sub-tropical regions of eastern Australia. The only native palm of the southeastern part of the continent, this species lacks a crownshaft and has a somewhat spherical, dark-green crown with drooping tips to the leaves, and a skirt of dead leaves usually hanging beneath the crown.

Trunk Grey to brownish-grey, to 30 m tall and 50 cm diameter, fairly stout and often swollen at the base. It is rough with close vertical fissures and ringed with incomplete horizontal leaf scars. Parts of the fibrous leaf bases sometimes remain attached to sections of the trunk.

Leaves Fan-shaped and glossy dark-green on both surfaces, with a short midrib visible on the back of the leaf. Leaf blades are 1-1.8 m across on stout, erect or curved stalks, to 3 m long. They are broadly circular in outline, pleated and divided about two-thirds the way down into 30-50 narrow, pointed segments with slender, entire or forked, drooping tips. The segments are thin-textured and fairly stiff, with a prominent central vein, raised below, and 6-7 longitudinal veins. Leaf stalks are flattened above and convex below, dull dark-green, often with white scurf below, about 2 cm diameter at the tip and 6 cm across at the base, where they become concave above and partially sheath the trunk. The sheathing bases consist of mats of fibres wrapped around the trunk with a pale, parchment-like tongue hanging down on the side opposite the leaf stalk. Younger, vigorously growing specimens are armed with short, pale-green, mostly downward-pointing spines along the margins of the lower half of the leaf stalk.

Inflorescence A long, pendulous, much-branched panicle, slightly shorter than the leaf stalks and arising from the leaf bases within the crown. Up to 1.5 m long, the thick, main stem is initially enclosed in several overlapping brown, woolly, sheathing bracts, 15-25 cm long. The flowers are borne in dense masses on numerous thin, pendulous branchlets. A number of inflorescences are usually present at the same time.

Flowers Yellow to cream, stalkless, 3-5 mm across with 3 blunt sepals and 3 fleshy, pointed petals about 3 mm long. They are bisexual with 6 short stamens with flattened filaments, a short style, minute stigma, and a 3-celled ovary containing one ovule in each cell. The flowers are borne singly or in small clusters, and densely packed along the branchlets of the inflorescence.

Fruits Dull reddish-brown to purplish-black when ripe, globular, almost stalkless, 16-20 mm diameter and quite hard, comprising a single spherical seed about 12 mm diameter with a papery covering surrounded by a thin fleshy layer.

Habitat Naturally occurring in warm temperate to tropical rainforests, in wet eucalypt forests and in more open situations, preferring low, moist areas. They commonly grow in swamps or seasonally wet sites in the north, and along stream banks and alluvial flats in the southern part of their range, preferring frost-free areas, although they will tolerate mild frosts. The trees grow best in well drained organically rich soils and will adapt to a wide variety of soil types, preferring shady sites when young. The fresh seed germinates within 3 months.

Distribution Widely distributed along a narrow coastal strip from Fraser Island in Qld through NSW to far eastern Vic.

Family Arecaceae.

Livistona benthamii   **Fan Palm**

The Fan Palm is a medium-sized, single-stemmed, fan-leaved palm of the coastal rainforests of the far north of Australia and New Guinea. This species lacks a crownshaft and has a large crown extending well down from the top of the trunk, comprising numerous bright, shiny-green fronds on long prickly stalks, with a skirt of dead fronds usually hanging from the top of the slender trunk.

Trunk Brown turning grey to dark grey with age, to 16 m tall and 40 cm diameter. In younger specimens the trunks are covered with the persistent remains of the old, bulbous leaf bases, which are eventually shed as the palm matures to leave a smooth trunk with horizontal leaf scars. The base of the trunk may retain the leaf bases for many years.

Leaves Glossy dark-green on both surfaces, fan-shaped, 2-3 m long, including the stalk which is 1-1.8 m long and 3-4 cm across at the base. The leaf blade is almost orbicular, 1-1.6 m long, deeply-divided and prominently pleated, with a noticeable thin and brittle, collar-like extension of the tip of the leaf stalk about 3 cm long. The leaves are divided more than two-thirds the way down (often almost to the midrib) into some 75-80 narrow segments, each about 25 mm wide at the base, with a prominent midvein and 8-10 secondary veins. The segments taper to long, fine, deeply forked, bristle-like, drooping tips. The leaf stalks are flattened with a slight ridge above and are convex below. They are dark-green with whitish scales on both surfaces, and a yellow stripe runs along the margins which are armed along the lower half with stout, curved or straight, dark-brown spines. The lower part of the leaf stalk produces masses of brown fibres along the margins, and expands into a large fibrous base that partially sheaths the trunk.

Inflorescence A branched panicle to 2 m or more long, arising from the leaf bases within the upper part of the crown. Several inflorescences are usually present at the same time. They have a thick stalk about 40 cm long and 6 cm across at the base, initially enclosed in brown, blunt bracts about 30 cm long.

Flowers Cream to pale-yellow, very small, 1-3 mm across, and borne in small clusters on the branchlets of the inflorescence. They are bisexual, with 3 sepals and 3 petals, 6 stamens with flattened filaments, and a 3-celled ovary with one ovule in each cell, tapering to a short style and minute stigma. Only one ovule develops into a seed. Flowering from May to August.

Fruits Bluish-black when ripe with a powdery bloom on the surface. They are globular to ovate with a constricted base, about 1 cm long, with a single, hard-shelled, globular seed about 6 mm across, surrounded by a thin, fleshy outer layer. Fruiting from September to November.

Habitat Naturally occurring in colonies in heavy black soils subject to seasonal flooding in lowland monsoon forests with permanent freshwater creeks, along the margins of paperbark swamps and in floodplains. They are slow growing, preferring shady sites in tropical and subtropical districts, although they will tolerate full sun when older. Fresh seed germinates in 3-4 months.

Distribution Coastal areas of northern NT around Darwin, the Alligator Rivers and Arnhem Land; the Cape York Peninsula in Qld and adjacent islands, extending into New Guinea.

Family Arecaceae.

Livistona decipiens   **Weeping Cabbage or Ribbon Fan Palm**

This attractive palm is a tall, single-stemmed, fan-leaved palm of the open forests of northeastern Australia, and has a pronounced, weeping appearance. It lacks a crownshaft and has a large, rounded crown of finely divided fronds with long, drooping tips.

Trunk Brown turning grey with age, to 15 m tall and 25 cm diameter. It is rough with small vertical fissures and an enlarged base, tapers gradually towards the top, and is prominently ringed with closely-spaced horizontal leaf scars. Some specimens retain their old leaf bases for many years.

Leaves Glossy dark-green to pale yellowish-green on both surfaces, fan-shaped with a midrib about 30 cm long. They are up to 4 m long including the straight stalks which may be up to 3 m long. The leaf blades are stiff and thin-textured, almost orbicular, about 1.5 m from the tip of the leaf stalk, and about 2 m diameter, strongly ribbed and pleated. They are divided to within 5 cm or less of the midrib into 70-80 narrow segments about 1 m long and 2-3 cm wide at their bases. Each segment is divided for about half its length into 2 very fine, pointed tips that hang vertically to give the frond a wilted, curtain-like appearance. The leaf stalks are flat above and convex below, about 25 mm wide at the tip and 5-7 cm wide at the base, and initially covered with circular flat grey scales below. Their margins are armed with numerous small, brown, curved spines, 3-5 mm long, closely-spaced along the bottom two-thirds of the leaf stalk. They have sheathing bases consisting of mats of fibres wrapped around the trunk.

Inflorescence A loose, much-branched panicle longer than the leaf stalks and shorter than the whole leaves, arched with a drooping tip. Several inflorescences are usually present at the same time. They comprise a stout, flattened stalk arising from the leaf bases within the crown and splitting into a small number of side branches that further divide into numerous slender, flowering branchlets, 10-15 cm long. The inflorescences are sheathed in the bud stage by deciduous overlapping bracts.

Flowers Bright yellow, very small, 1-3 mm across with a solid, fleshy base, arranged in densely-packed small clusters along the slender branchlets of the inflorescence, on very short stalks which lengthen in fruit to about 1 cm long. The flowers are bisexual with 3 sepals and 3 fleshy, blunt petals, 6 stamens with flattened filaments, a 3-celled ovary with one ovule in each cell, a short style and minute stigma. Only one ovule develops into a seed.

Fruits Shiny black when ripe, spherical, 12-18 mm across on stalks to 1 cm long. They comprise a single, spherical seed about 1 cm diameter, surrounded by a very thin, fleshy layer and a minutely-wrinkled outer coat.

Habitat Naturally occurring in small scattered colonies, often along stream banks in open eucalypt forests and rainforest margins, preferring sandy soil with readily available ground water. Fresh seed germinates easily within 4 months and they will grow from the tropics to warm temperate areas, preferring a sunny site with plenty of water.

Distribution Widely distributed along the central coast of Qld from just south of Gladstone to Townsville.

Family Arecaceae.

Livistona drudei

This uncommon palm is fast losing its native habitats due to land clearing and the draining of wetlands. It is a tall, single-stemmed, fan-leaved palm of the open forests of coastal northeastern Australia. It lacks a crownshaft and has a spreading, fairly open crown of finely divided, bright, shiny-green fronds with drooping tips on stiff, spiny stalks, extending well down from the top of the trunk.

Trunk Straight with a bulbous base. The trunk is brown in younger specimens and often covered with persistent, dark-brown to black leaf bases. Old specimens have pale-grey, smooth trunks, to 20 m tall and 25 cm diameter, and ringed with closely-spaced horizontal leaf scars.

Leaves Bright shiny green on both surfaces, fan-shaped with a midrib about 35 cm long extending from the end of the leaf stalk. The leaves are up to 4 m long, including the stalks which are up to 3 m long. The leaf blades are thin-textured and stiff, almost orbicular, about 1.5 m across, strongly-ribbed and pleated, and divided more than half way down into numerous narrow segments about 8 mm wide at their bases, with thin, deeply-forked, drooping and frayed tips. The leaf stalks are pale to dark-green, flattish above and convex below, 5-7 cm across at their brown to purplish-black bases, and tapering to about 2 cm wide at the tip. The margins of the lower half of the stalk are armed with closely-spaced, curved, black spines, and the sheathing bases consist of mats of fibres wrapped around the trunk.

Inflorescence A loose, much-branched arching panicle, shorter than the leaf stalks, to about 1 m long. Several inflorescences are usually present at the same time. They arise from the leaf bases within the top of the crown, and are sheathed in bud by a series of overlapping tubular bracts.

Flowers Cream, very small, 1-2 mm across, solitary or borne in small clusters along the branchlets of the inflorescence. They are bisexual with 3 petals and 3 sepals, 6 stamens with flattened filaments, a 3-celled ovary with one ovule in each cell, a short style and minute stigma. Only one ovule develops into a seed.

Fruits Shiny black when ripe, globular, 11-15 mm long, with a single globular seed about 9 mm across, surrounded by a fleshy, fibrous outer layer.

Habitat Naturally occurring in small colonies along stream banks and the margins of paperbark wetlands. Fresh seed germinates readily within 3 months, and the seedlings prefer partial shade and rich soil with plenty of water.

Distribution Restricted to a narrow coastal strip from Halifax Bay to the Mission Beach area in northeastern Qld, and Hinchinbrook Island.

Family Arecaceae.

Livistona humilis   **Sand Palm**

The Sand Palm is a dwarf, single-stemmed, fan-leaved palm of the open forests of northern Australia and the adjacent islands. This distinctive palm lacks a crownshaft and has a fairly sparse and spreading crown of bright green fronds on long, prickly stalks, with a skirt of dead fronds usually hanging down around the slender trunk.

Trunk Grey to dark-brown or blackish, covered with the persistent bases of the dead fronds, or ringed with horizontal leaf scars, and often blackened by fire. The trunk is usually 2-5 m tall and 8-12 cm diameter, although some very old specimens may reach 6 m.

Leaves Bright shiny-green above and slightly paler below, fan-shaped, 1-1.3 m long including the stalk which may be 40-90 cm long and about 3 cm across at the base, tapering to about 15 mm at the tip. The leaf blade is almost orbicular, 30-80 cm diameter, pleated longitudinally from the base and divided about two-thirds the way down into 30-40 narrow segments with 3-4 main veins. The segments are 15-20 mm wide at the base and taper to long, fine, forked and thread-like tips. The leaf stalks are flattened above and convex below, and armed along the margins with small, forward-pointing spines. Their sheathing bases consist of mats of fibres wrapped around the trunk with a pale, parchment-like tongue hanging down on the side opposite the leaf stalk.

Inflorescence A long, slender, erect to slightly arching, loose panicle, 1-2 m long with a smooth, stiff stalk, 1-1.5 m long, and many small, flower-bearing branchlets. Several inflorescences are usually present at the same time, arising from the base of the upper fronds and projecting above the crown.

Flowers Pale-yellow, very small, 2-4 mm across with 3 short, thin, broadly-triangular sepals, and 3 thick, oblong petals. The flowers are solitary or arranged in stalkless clusters of 3-5 flowers along the small branches of the inflorescence. They are bisexual and the stamens are united at their bases to form a deep cup around the ovary, which has a short, conical style. Flowering from September to May.

Fruits Green turning shiny purplish-black when mature. They are ovoid with a constricted base, 10-17 mm long, and consist of an ovoid, somewhat flattened seed about 1 cm long, surrounded by a fleshy outer layer. Fruiting from January to July.

Habitat A common understorey palm of the open eucalypt forests and woodlands in the wetter parts of northern Australia, preferring sandy soils with groundwater available, often forming pure stands or scattered colonies. They are slow growing and large specimens are impossible to transplant. Fresh seed germinates within 6 months.

Distribution Widespread in the Victoria River district, Arnhem Land and the Darwin to Katherine areas of the NT, Melville Island, and northeastern WA.

Family Arecaceae.

Livistona inermis

A small to medium-sized, single-stemmed, fan-leaved palm growing in open forests of northern Australia. It lacks a crownshaft and has an open crown of finely divided, stiff and spiky, pale, greyish-green fronds without drooping tips on slender stalks. A skirt of dead fronds usually hangs from the top of the trunk.

Trunk Reddish-brown turning grey with age, to 8 m tall and 12 cm diameter, straight, ringed with prominent, pale, closely-spaced horizontal leaf scars. The trunk often retains fibrous leaf bases in parts, giving it an untidy appearance.

Leaves Dull, greyish-green on both surfaces, fan-shaped with a short midrib, to 2 m long including the stalks which are 0.4-1.2 m long. The leaves are divided almost down to the midrib into stiff, spreading, slender segments, 60-80 cm long and 5-10 mm wide. The segments fork about one third of the way down into 2 long, pointed tips, and have a tessellated appearance, with numerous prominent veins connected by short transverse veinlets. The leaf stalks are flattened above and ridged below, pale-green and scurfy below, about 2 cm across at the base, and tapering to about 1 cm wide at the tip. Their margins are sharp, and armed with small black spines near the base. The bases consist of mats of fibres wrapped around the trunk with a parchment-like tongue hanging down on the side opposite the leaf stalk.

Inflorescence A sparsely-branched, drooping panicle, shorter than the leaves, 25-45 cm long, with a thick stalk, branched 3-4 times into smaller panicles with many short, thick, flower-bearing branchlets. Several inflorescences are usually present at the same time, arising from the leaf bases within the crown and sheathed in bud by a series of pale-brown overlapping tubular bracts.

Flowers Cream to yellow, 2-3 mm across, solitary, borne on short stalks along the branchlets of the inflorescence. They are bisexual with 3 thin, broadly-ovate petals and 6 stamens united at their bases. They have a 3-celled ovary with one ovule in each cell, a short conical style and minute stigma. Only one ovule develops into a seed.

Fruits Red-brown to violet or black when ripe, ovoid, 10-15 mm long and 6-10 mm across, with a single ovoid seed surrounded by a slightly fleshy outer layer.

Habitat Naturally occurring on sandstone outcrops and escarpments in open forests and along the coastal plains. Fresh seed germinates slowly and sporadically within 9 months. The seedlings are slow growing and difficult to establish.

Distribution Endemic to the NT in the Katherine, Alligator Rivers, Arnhem Land regions, and the Sir Edward Pellow Group of islands in the Gulf of Carpentaria.

Family Arecaceae.

Livistona loriphylla

This very slender palm is similar to *Livistona inermis*. It is a small, single-stemmed, fan-leaved palm of the open forests of the Kimberley region of northwestern Australia. It lacks a crownshaft and has a sparse, open crown of finely-divided bright, shiny-green fronds with drooping tips on slender stalks with prickly margins. A few dead fronds are usually hanging from the top of the trunk.

Trunk Dark greyish-brown, to 8 m tall and 12 cm diameter and may be blackened by fire. It is smooth and straight with a swollen base, and ringed with closely-spaced horizontal leaf scars. This species does not retain the old leaf bases on the trunk.

Leaves Bright shiny-green, fan-shaped with a short midrib, to 2 m long including the stalks which are up to 1.2 m long. The leaves are divided almost down to the midrib into about 30 stiff, spreading, slender segments, 60-80 cm long and about 12 mm wide at their bases. They are divided again about half way down into 2 long, pointed, drooping tips. The leaf stalks are pale-green, flattened above and ridged below, about 3 cm across at the base, and taper to about 2 cm wide at the tip. Their margins are sharp, and towards the base of the stalk are armed with small spines. The sheathing bases consist of mats of fibres wrapped around the trunk, with a parchment-like tongue hanging down on the side opposite the leaf stalk.

Inflorescence A fairly dense, drooping panicle, shorter than the leaves. It grows to about 80 cm long and has a thick stalk, divided 3-4 times into many slender, flower-bearing branchlets up to 20 cm long. Several inflorescences are usually present at the same time, arising from the leaf bases within the crown and sheathed in bud by a series of pale-brown, overlapping, tubular bracts.

Flowers Cream, very small and stalkless, about 2 mm across, borne in small clusters along the branchlets of the inflorescence. They are bisexual with 3 thick, pointed petals, 3 broad sepals, and 6 stamens united into a shallow cup at their bases. They have a 3-celled ovary with one ovule in each cell, a short style and minute stigma. Only one ovule develops into a seed.

Fruits Dull black when ripe, obovoid, about 12 mm long with a single, globular seed surrounded by a fleshy, fibrous outer layer.

Habitat Naturally occurring in small colonies in open forests where grass fires are common. The fresh seed germinates slowly and sporadically within 9 months. The seedlings are slow-growing and difficult to establish.

Distribution Found only in the Kimberley region of northwestern WA.

Family Arecaceae.

Livistona mariae   Red or Central Australian Cabbage Palm

This tall, single-stemmed, fan-leaved palm is confined to an isolated valley in the arid centre of northern Australia: the remnant population of a species that flourished when the climate was much wetter. It lacks a crownshaft, and has a dense, compact, spherical crown of pale, greyish-green fronds with drooping tips, and a skirt of dead fronds hanging from the top of the slender trunk.

Trunk Pale to dark-grey, to 20 m tall and 40 cm diameter. The trunk tapers slightly towards the top from a swollen base which often retains a few scattered remnants of the old leaf bases. The rest of the trunk is smooth and ringed with horizontal leaf scars.

Leaves The leaves of young plants are tinged with red, hence the common name. Mature leaves are shiny-green above, grey-green and waxy below. They are fan-shaped, erect to spreading and drooping, to 4.5 m long including the long, straight stalks which are up to 2 m long. The leaf blades are stiff and thick, almost orbicular, to 3 m diameter, strongly ribbed and prominently pleated. They are divided more than half way down into numerous, linear, pointed segments, about 25 mm wide at the base, with entire or frayed, drooping tips. The leaf stalks are flat above and convex below, 3-4 cm wide at the tip, expanded at the base to partially encircle the trunk, and are armed with small spines along the lower margins. Their sheathing bases consist of mats of fibres wrapped around the trunk with a pale, parchment-like tongue hanging down on the side opposite the leaf stalk.

Inflorescence A loose, much-branched, drooping panicle, shorter than the leaf stalks. Several inflorescences are usually present at the same time. They are up to 1.3 m long with stout stalks arising from the leaf bases within the crown, and are sheathed in bud by a number of overlapping, blunt, tubular bracts, 15-30 cm long.

Flowers Greenish-yellow, about 5 mm across and bisexual, arranged in dense clusters on the branchlets of the inflorescence. They have 3 sepals and 3 petals, 6 distinct stamens with thick, flattened filaments, and a 3-celled ovary with one ovule in each cell, tapering to a short style. Only one ovule develops into a seed.

Fruits Glossy black when ripe, globular, 15-20 mm across, comprising a single globular seed surrounded by a thin, fleshy outer layer.

Habitat Occurs in a single, isolated area, forming colonies around permanent waterholes and soaks in hot, arid country in open sites. Its survival in this habitat depends on a continual seepage of water into this otherwise dry area. Fresh seed germinates erratically within 6 months, and the plants prefer well-drained soil with plenty of water. They are quite slow-growing but can be grown in tropical, subtropical and temperate areas, and will withstand full sun.

Distribution Restricted to the Finke River and its tributaries in the MacDonnell Ranges of southern NT. Widely cultivated in parks and gardens as far south as Melbourne.

Family Arecaceae.

Livistona muelleri   **Dwarf Fan Palm**

The Dwarf Fan Palm is a small, single-stemmed, fan-leaved palm of the open forests and grasslands of northeastern Australia and New Guinea. This attractive, small-growing species lacks a crown-shaft and has a compact, dense crown of stiff, dark-green fronds with prickly stalks, closely packed around the upper part of the trunk. Dead fronds often hang down around the top of the trunk, although they are frequently burnt off by bushfires.

Trunk Dark-brown to black, to 3 m tall and 50 cm diameter. It is covered with the brown, fibrous bases of the old leaf stalks and the remains of the stalks themselves, although they may be burnt off by fires.

Leaves Glossy dark-green above and paler or greyish-green below. They are fan-shaped, to 2 m long, including their straight stalks which may be over 1 m long. The leaf blades are stiff and thick, almost orbicular, and measure 80-90 cm from the tip of the leaf stalk. Strongly-ribbed and prominently pleated, they are divided about two-thirds the way down into about 50 linear segments with depressed midveins. The leaf segments are up to 4 cm wide at their bases and taper to pointed, shortly forked, thread-like tips. The margins of the leaf segments are turned up, and may be minutely serrated. The leaf stalks are pale to dark-green with brownish scurf on both surfaces, especially when young They are flat above and convex below, about 5-6 cm wide at the base and 2 cm wide at the tip, which forms a thin, brown-tipped, brittle, raised collar on the upper surface of the leaf blade. The lower parts of the margins of the leaf stalks are armed with curved, mostly downward-pointing yellow spines with black tips, about 5 mm long, becoming smaller towards the top of the stalk. The sheathing bases of the leaf stalks consist of mats of fibres wrapped around the trunk.

Inflorescence A loose panicle, shorter than the leaves, to 1.3 m long. It has a stout stalk about 40 cm long, and numerous small, flower-bearing branchlets. A number of inflorescences are usually present at the same time, arising from the leaf bases within the crown. They are initially enclosed in pointed bracts, 20-30 cm long, that are shed before the flowers open.

Flowers Yellow, very small, 1-3 mm across, solitary or in small clusters along the slender branchlets of the inflorescence. They are bisexual with 3 sepals and 3 petals, 6 stamens with flattened filaments, a 3-celled ovary with one erect ovule in each cell, a short style and minute stigma. Only one ovule develops into a seed.

Fruits Black with a bluish bloom when ripe. They are spherical to ovate, 6-11 mm long with a short stalk about 2 mm long. They comprise a single, globular seed, about 6 mm across with a wrinkled skin, surrounded by a thin, slightly fleshy layer.

Habitat Naturally occurring in scattered colonies in open forests and grasslands. This very slow-growing palm will tolerate full sun and grow in tropical and warm subtropical regions. Fresh seed germinates sporadically and may take up to 8 months.

Distribution Northern Qld, from Cairns to the tip of the Cape York Peninsula, extending into New Guinea, and cultivated in frost-free areas as far south as Sydney.

Family Arecaceae.

Livistona rigida

A medium-sized to tall, single-stemmed, fan-leaved palm growing in dense colonies along some of the inland, northerly-flowing rivers of northern Australia. This attractive, hardy species has reddish young fronds, lacks a crownshaft, and has a large, fairly open, spreading crown of dull, bluish-green fronds with slightly drooping tips and long, arching stalks. A skirt of dead fronds usually hangs from the top of the trunk.

Trunk Brown to dark-grey, to 20 m tall and 40 cm diameter. It is smooth and ringed with prominent, closely-spaced, horizontal leaf scars.

Leaves Bluish-green on both surfaces. New growth is tinged with yellow or red, and the seedlings are reddish. They are fan-shaped with a short midrib, to 4 m long, including the 1-2 m long straight stalks. The leaf blades are stiff and thick, 1-1.5 m across, strongly-ribbed and prominently-pleated. They are divided more than one-third the way down into numerous linear, pointed segments to 3 cm wide at the base and tapering to long, forked, thread-like tips. The leaf stalks are pale-green to yellowish, flat above and convex below, about 8 cm across at the base, tapering to 3 cm across at the tip and armed with stout spines along the margins. Their sheathing bases consist of mats of fibres wrapped around the trunk.

Inflorescence A loose, much-branched, semi-erect panicle arising from the leaf bases within the crown. It is 1-2 m long with short, rigid branches and a stout stalk up to 1 m long. A number of inflorescences may be present at the same time. They are sheathed in bud by overlapping, blunt, tubular bracts.

Flowers Yellow, very small, 1-3 mm across and bisexual. They are stalkless and arranged in groups of 3-5 on the branchlets of the inflorescence. They have 3 thick-textured petals and 3 sepals, 6 distinct stamens with thick, flattened filaments, and a 3-celled ovary with one ovule in each cell, tapering into a short style. Only one ovule develops into a seed. Flowering in August and September.

Fruits Purple-black when ripe, hard and globular, 1-2 cm across, comprising a single, hard-shelled seed surrounded by a thin, fleshy outer layer. Fruiting in January and February.

Habitat Naturally occurring along inland waterways, in monsoon forests, often forming large colonies in fairly open situations on deep, moist, clay soils. Fresh seed germinates within 3 months. They are very hardy and will grow in tropical, subtropical and temperate areas, and inland in clay soils with a good water supply in the dry periods.

Distribution Locally common along the Gregory River and its tributaries in northwestern Qld, and in the Roper River district of the NT.

Family Arecaceae.

Pandanus aquaticus
River Pandanus

River Pandanus is a medium-sized, clumping, palm-like tree with numerous prop roots around the base of the trunk. This species is found along freshwater pools, swamps and creeks of northern Australia. It has long, sword-like, drooping, bluish-green leaves, spirally arranged to form relatively large, dense crowns at the ends of the branches, with many dead leaves hanging down.

Trunk Pinkish-brown, turning light-grey, to 5 m tall and 15-20 cm diameter, branching near the top. It is smooth and ringed with closely-spaced, deeply-ridged horizontal leaf scars. New stems arise from the base to form dense clumps, and numerous slender prop roots descend from the base of the trunk to anchor the plant to the bottom of quite deep pools.

Leaves Dull, bluish-green on both surfaces, thick and leathery, sword-like with long, pointed tips and broad, fibrous bases partially sheathing the top of the trunk. They are spirally arranged to form a tufted crown with drooping tips, 1.2-2.7 m long and 3-8 cm wide, widest at the base. The leaves have numerous fine, longitudinal veins, and are M-shaped in cross section, being deeply-channelled above with a prominent, raised midrib below, and gently curling margins. The midrib is armed along the midsection of the underside of the leaf blade with ascending prickles, 2-3 mm long and 18-35 mm apart. The margins bear small, reddish-tipped, ascending prickles, 1.5-3.5 mm long, beginning about 6 cm from the leaf base and becoming much smaller towards the tip, which is almost unarmed.

Flowers Creamy-white, small and inconspicuous, produced on separate male and female plants. Male flowers consist entirely of stamens, closely-packed in yellowish, stalkless, terminal, cylindrical spikes, 3-6 cm long and 12-15 mm diameter. They are borne in the axils of pale, pointed, leafy bracts to 31 cm long and 3 cm wide with prickly margins. Female flowers are solitary, ellipsoid heads of densely packed ovaries, each containing a single ovule, topped by a pointed stigma and style. They are produced in the centre of the leafy crowns, and expand after fertilisation to form a large fruiting body.

Fruits Pineapple-like, 3-sided, broadly-spherical clusters, 7-13 cm diameter, of more than 100 closely-packed drupes attached to a central core. At maturity they are still green, and the core shrinks within a few days, causing the drupes to fall in a mass. Individual drupes turn pale yellow-orange to brown when ripe. The majority are single-celled, 7-11 mm wide and 6-8 mm thick, with 5-6 smooth, gently-curving, shiny sides. They have a rounded, pyramidal outer tip bearing the 2 mm long pointed remains of the stigma, and taper to a fibrous inner base. A few drupes are 2-celled, 10-14 mm wide with 2 pointed tips. They contain a single, barrel-shaped seed in each cell, 7-8 mm long, surrounded by a tough outer coat.

Habitat Found along the margins of creeks, swamps and pools. They often grow under palms, and prefer the shallows beside deep pools where they anchor themselves to the bottom with prop roots. White cockatoos and turtles feed on the fruits.

Distribution Common in northern Australia along lowland waterways from northwestern Qld to northern NT and northeastern WA.

Family Pandanaceae.

Pandanus gemmifer

A medium-sized, slender, palm-like tree with prop roots around the base of the trunk, growing in the rainforests of northeastern Australia. This unusual plant has long, slender branches bearing spirals of small, tufted plantlets. The plantlets form grass-like clumps some distance below the crown of long, spiny, arching, sword-like leaves. The plantlets fall to the ground when mature and take root, eventually growing into new trees.

Trunk Pale-brown, smooth with scattered low, rounded, warty projections. It is up to 8 m tall and 15 cm diameter, with prop roots around the base, although these are often quite short.

Leaves Dark-green on both surfaces, thick and leathery, sword-like with long, pointed tips and broad, fibrous bases partially sheathing the top of the trunk. They are spirally arranged to form a tufted crown with drooping tips. The leaves are up to 2.5 m long and about 5 cm wide for most of their length. They are M-shaped in cross section, being deeply-channelled above with a prominent, raised midrib below, and slightly curling margins. The lower half of the midrib is armed with small, forward-pointing spines about 1.5 mm long. The leaf margins bear forward-pointing, brown-tipped spines to 4 mm long near the base. The spines on the margins and midrib become shorter and more closely-spaced towards the tip of the leaf blade. Leafy sprouts are produced below the crown in a series of 3 spirals in opposite directions. The first spiral is a series of buds, the next bears leafy sprouts with 6-15 leaves, 3-7 cm long and 3-4 mm wide, the third spiral is a series of older sprouts each with about 43 leaves, 22-45 cm long and 4-12 mm wide, with ascending prickles along the margins and midrib. The latter fall to the ground when mature.

Flowers Produced on separate male and female plants. Male plants have not been studied, and vegetative propagation by the small plantlets seems to be responsible for much of their reproductive capacity. Female flowers are solitary ovoid heads of densely-packed ovaries each containing a single ovule, produced on long stalks in the centre of the leafy crowns, and expanding to form a large fruiting body.

Fruits Pineapple-like ovoid clusters, 20-25 cm long and 10-18 cm across, comprising about 40 closely packed segments. They are green turning deep-red when ripe, with a long, pendulous stalk to 50 cm long and 2 cm diameter. The fruiting body eventually separates into its component segments. The segments are 32-56 mm long and 29-40 mm wide across the top, and about 4-5 cm deep, with a constricted, pale, fibrous base. Each segment has 4-6 sides and a shiny, hard, tough, domed upper surface with 8-17 crowded, slender, pointed tips to 4 mm long in the centre, corresponding to the number of single-seeded carpels making up the segment. They have a tough outer coat surrounding a fleshy and fibrous inner layer, with spindle-shaped seeds, 13-15 mm long and 3-4 mm diameter, embedded in it.

Habitat Grows along the banks of creeks and watercourses and in wet sites in lowland and highland tropical rainforests.

Distribution Found in scattered colonies along the coast and tablelands of tropical northeastern Qld.

Family Pandanaceae.

Pandanus monticola

A medium-sized, shrubby pandan growing as an understorey species in the tropical rainforests of northeastern Australia. This species has a number of branching stems arising forming a tufted clump, each terminating in a plume of long, arching, strap-like leaves with spiny margins, and giving rise to brilliant-red, globular fruiting bodies.

Trunk Erect to semi-erect, branching towards the top, often weighed-down by its leaves and the surrounding vegetation. The trunk is brownish-grey, 1-3 m tall and 25-50 mm diameter, smooth, ringed with wavy leaf scars and dotted with small, warty projections. The base bears small prop roots and is usually obscured by numerous leafy suckers.

Leaves Dull, pale-green on both surfaces, thick and leathery, strap-like with long, pointed tips and broad, fibrous bases partially sheathing the top of the trunk. The leaves are arranged in 3 tight spirals forming a tufted crown with long, hanging tips. They are up to 2.5 m long and 4 cm wide at the base in the more vigorously-growing younger specimens, although in older plants they are usually 1.2-2 m long. The leaves are M-shaped in cross section, being deeply-channelled above with gently curling margins and a prominent midrib raised below. The margins and midrib are armed with small, forward-pointing spines, 1-2 mm long. The spines become shorter with broader bases towards the tip of the leaf blade.

Flowers Produced on separate male and female plants. The males consist entirely of stamens closely packed in stalkless, cylindrical spikes, 5-7 cm long and 15-20 mm diameter. They are borne along a terminal stalk in the axils of long, leafy bracts to about 10 cm long. Female flowers comprise globular heads of densely packed ovaries each containing a single ovule topped by a long, pointed stigma and style. They are produced in the centre of the crowns, surrounded by deciduous leafy bracts to about 65 cm long, and expand after fertilisation to form a large fruiting body.

Fruits Globular to ovoid clusters of tightly packed pointed drupes, 6-10 cm across with spiny stalks to 50 cm long and about 1 cm diameter. They are green turning bright-red when ripe, and arise from the leaf bases within the crowns at the ends of the stems. The fruiting body slowly disintegrates at maturity releasing the small, sharply-pointed drupes. Individual drupes are 2-3 cm long and 2-3 mm across, linear to oblong with a sharp, upward-pointing tip and a single seed embedded in a pithy inner layer.

Habitat Grows in tropical rainforests, usually along the banks of creeks and waterways, from sea-level to cool, highland areas.

Distribution Found along the coast and tablelands of tropical northeastern Qld.

Family Pandanaceae.

Pandanus spiralis

The Screw Palm is a moderately large, palm-like tree with small prop roots around the base of the trunk. This pandan often retains the old leaf bases which form a distinctive spiral around the trunk. It produces compact crowns of long, prickly, sword-like leaves, spirally-arranged at the ends of the branches, with brown dead leaves hanging from the base of the crown to form a skirt around the top of the trunk.

Trunk Brown, turning grey in the older parts, to 12 m tall and 20 cm diameter, usually forked towards the top. It has a slightly decumbent base with short, thick, prop roots. The leaf bases may remain attached to the trunk in a spiral arrangement for some time. They fall to leave a woody surface banded with pale leaf scars and bearing small, ascending, flattened rootlets. These rootlets grow in the leaf bases and absorb nutrients from collected debris.

Leaves Dull mid-green on both surfaces with a slightly whitish bloom, thick and leathery, sword-like with long, pointed tips and broad, fibrous bases partially sheathing the top of the trunk. The leaves are arranged in 3 distinct, tight spirals, forming a tufted crown with drooping tips. They may be up to 3 m long and 10 cm wide at the base in luxuriant younger specimens, although they are usually 1.5-2 m long and 4-8 cm wide. The leaves are M-shaped in cross section, being deeply channelled above with a prominent midrib raised below, and gently curling margins. The midrib is armed with small, black-tipped, backward and forward pointing spines, the margins bear small forward-pointing spines 2-3 mm long. The spines become shorter and more widely spaced towards the tip of the leaf blade.

Flowers Small, white, sweetly-scented and inconspicuous. They are produced on separate male and female plants. Male flowers consist entirely of stamens closely packed in stalkless, terminal, cylindrical spikes, 3-10 cm long and 30-35 mm diameter, borne in the axils of long, pointed, leafy bracts to about 30 cm long. Female flowers are solitary ovoid heads of densely-packed ovaries each containing a single ovule, produced in the centre of the leafy crowns, and expanding after fertilisation to form a large fruiting body.

Fruits Pineapple-like, ovoid clusters, 15-30 cm across, comprising 8-35 closely packed segments. They are green turning orange to red when ripe. The fruiting body disintegrates while still attached to the tree, and the segments fall separately to the ground. The segments are 5-10 cm long and 5-9 cm wide across the top, and about 5 cm deep with a slightly constricted base. They consist of a varying number of closely packed carpels, clearly visible on the outer surface of the segments. The carpels have a flattish outer surface with a scarcely prominent tip and taper to a fibrous inner base. They have a tough, hard, outer coat surrounding a fleshy and fibrous inner layer and 5-7 seeds. Fruiting from June to October.

Habitat Grows along the banks of creeks and watercourses, in swamps, lagoons and the fringes of floodplains; open forests, woodlands, coastal dunes and at the edges of coastal plains. The seeds germinate within about one month and are reasonably fast growing.

Distribution Common from northern WA through the NT, northern and northeastern Qld as far south as the tropic of Capricorn, extending into tropical Asia.

Family Pandanaceae.

Pandanus tectorius
(syn. P. pedunculatus)

Beach Pandan
Screw Pine

A medium-sized, crooked, branching pandan with prop roots and numerous cylindrical root-like extensions around the base of the trunk. Commonly seen along the central east coast of Australia in rainforest pockets and open sites, this distinctive tree bears tufted crowns of sword-like leaves at the ends of slender, crooked branches.

Trunk Pale-grey, erect, to 18 m tall and 20 cm diameter, although it usually grows to around 3-6 m tall, with stilt-like prop roots emerging from below the centre of the trunk. The prop roots are sometimes reduced to short, thick, cylindrical, root-like extensions around the base. The trunk is smooth, ringed with pale wavy leaf scars and dotted with small nodules, particularly on the prop roots, and branches a number of times in older specimens.

Leaves Dull mid-green to bluish-green above, with a whitish bloom below, thick and leathery, sword-like with long, pointed tips and broad, fibrous bases partially sheathing the top of the trunk. The leaves are typically spirally arranged in 4 rows, forming small, tufted crowns with erect to drooping tips. They are up to 1.5 m long and 5-10 cm wide at the base in younger, luxuriant specimens. They are M-shaped in cross section, being deeply-channelled above with a prominent midrib raised below, and gently curling margins. The midrib is smooth, or may have a few serrations in the lower part. The margins bear small, forward-pointing spines or serrations.

Flowers Produced on separate male and female plants. Male flowers consist entirely of stamens closely packed in white, terminal, cylindrical spikes, 8-10 cm long and 3-4 cm diameter, borne on stalks about twice as long in the axils of leafy bracts. Female flowers are solitary, ovoid heads of densely-packed ovaries each containing a single ovule, produced on thick stalks 5-12 cm long in the centre of the leafy crowns, and expanding after fertilisation to form a large fruiting body. Flowering throughout the year.

Fruits Pineapple-like, ovoid clusters, to 25 cm across, comprising up to about 50 closely-packed segments. They are green turning yellowish-brown when ripe. The fruiting body disintegrates when mature to release the separate segments. The segments are 4-6 cm long and 4-5 cm wide across the top, and about 8 cm deep with a constricted, fibrous, pale base. They consist of 7-18 (usually 8) closely packed carpels, clearly visible on the outer surface of the segments. The segments have a convex outer surface with a prominent, grey, pointed tip. They have a tough, hard outer coat surrounding a fleshy and fibrous inner layer containing a single, edible seed.

Habitat Grows in colonies along the coast, on beaches, in open sites, along waterways and the margins of the remaining coastal rainforest pockets.

Distribution Locally common from northeastern Qld along the coast as far south as Port Macquarie in NSW.

Family Pandanaceae.

Freycinetia excelsa Climbing Pandan

A long, slender, woody, climbing pandan found in rainforests of the tropical and subtropical east coast of Australia and New Guinea. This vigorous species clings to palms and tree trunks with small, wiry, adventitious roots arising along the stems. It is much-branched with closely-spaced, fairly stiff, stem-clasping leaves, and spirals around the tree, ascending to the top of the canopy, with its dark-green, prickly leaves standing out at right-angles to the trunk.

Stem Very long and wiry, branching freely, 7-10 mm diameter and covered with the spiralling leaf bases and their basal brown, papery bracts. It is greyish-brown, woody and ringed with closely-spaced leaf scars at the base.

Leaves Stiff and leathery, dark-green above and slightly paler below. They are linear to lanceo-late, 10-50 cm long and 6-10 mm wide, with long, pointed tips. The margins are curved under, and the midrib is deeply depressed on the upper surface to give the leaf an M-shaped cross section. The margins are armed with small, mostly forward-pointing pale spines, 1-2 mm long at the base of the leaf, and with very small prickles near the tip. The under surface of the midrib has tiny, relatively widely-spaced, forward-pointing, curved spines towards the tip of the leaf. The bases of the leaves partially sheath the stem and each is covered by a thin, papery, brown bract about 3 cm long with small teeth at the rounded tip and sometimes along the margins. The leaves have about 22 notice-able parallel veins, slightly raised below and extending the whole length of the leaf.

Flowers Produced on separate male and female plants. Male flowers consist entirely of stamens about 1 mm long, closely-packed in yellow to creamy-brown cylindrical spikes. They are 25-30 mm long and are borne singly or 2-3 together on terminal stalks about 2 cm long in the axils of orange to red ovate to lanceolate leafy bracts, 5-7 cm long and 25-35 mm wide. Female flowers are globular heads of densely-packed ovaries each containing numerous ovules, and topped by 2-3 stigmas. They are produced at the ends of the stems and are surrounded by deciduous red, fleshy, leafy bracts, 5-7 cm long and 25-35 mm wide. Flowering in early summer.

Fruits Ovoid to ovoid-oblong, 4-7 cm long and 2-4 cm across on brown stalks about 3 cm long and 5 mm diameter, made up of clusters of tightly packed berries. They are green turning bright-red to scarlet when ripe, and arise singly or in groups of up to 4 from the leaf bases at the ends of the stems. The fruiting body slowly disintegrates releasing the small, pointed berries. These are 3-7 mm long, club-shaped, with a pyramidal tip, 2-3 mm long, flattened with 2-4 pointed yellowish stigmas, and containing numerous small seeds.

Habitat Grows in tropical and subtropical rainforests, forming large, straggling clumps on tree trunks, and scrambling over rocks.

Distribution Locally common along the coast, from the Tweed Valley of far northern NSW to northeastern Qld and New Guinea.

Family Pandanaceae.

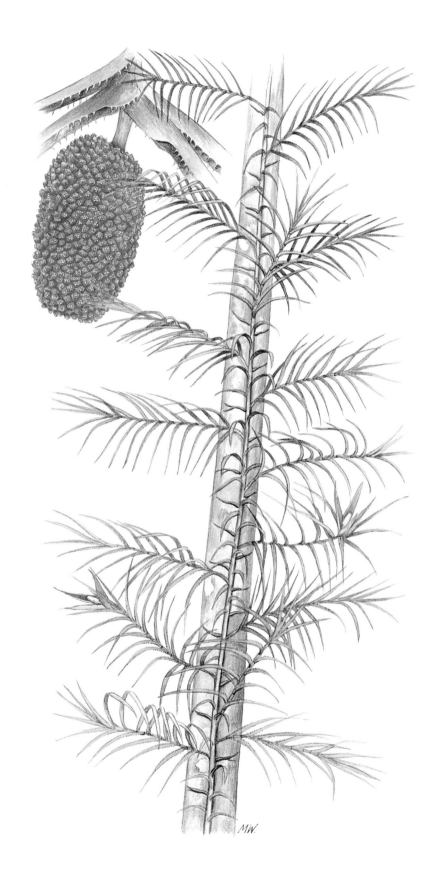

Cycas armstrongii   **Bulumara**

The Bulumara is a medium-sized, slender, palm-like cycad found in the stunted, open forests of northern Australia. This widespread species has an erect to spreading crown of leathery, dark-green leaves emerging from the top of the trunk. The plants defoliate completely after fire and in cool conditions, eventually producing spectacular flushes of bright green new leaves.

Trunk Dark-grey to brownish-black, to 4 m tall and 10-15 cm diameter, usually unbranched, although it may occasionally fork. It is woody and covered with closely-packed, small, pale to dark-grey, triangular to ovate leaf scars.

Leaves Soft and leathery, glossy, pale to dark-green above, dull and slightly paler below, and pinnately divided into 100-180 forward and slightly upward-pointing leaflets. The whole leaf is 0.5-1.2 m long and 20-26 cm across with a short, slender, cylindrical stalk to 25 cm long and 1 cm diameter, with a bulbous base, armed with backward-pointing, regularly-spaced brown-tipped spines about 4 mm long along the margins. The leaflets are linear to slightly sickle-shaped, 7-14 cm long and 5-10 mm wide, flat with sharply-pointed yellowish-brown tips and narrowed bases. They are opposite, regularly spaced with a prominent yellow midrib, depressed above and raised on the undersurface of the leaflet, causing the margins to curl slightly under. The leaflets are longest at the centre of the leaf, smaller at the tip and base. Young leaves are bright yellowish-green, covered with downy hairs with the leaflets folded together.

Cones Unisexual, stalkless, borne singly in the centre of the crown on separate male and female plants. The male cone is ovoid, rusty-brown and downy outside, 12-20 cm long, with many tightly-packed, spirally-arranged, hard, scale-like segments. These are wedge-shaped with a point on the outside, bearing hundreds of tiny, pollen-bearing capsules on the flat undersurface. Male cones open when mature to release large quantities of wind-borne pollen. Female cones are dome-shaped, about 10 cm across, with numerous flattened, triangular, scale-like segments with long, sharp, pointed tips, serrated margins and 2 lobes at the base. They open early to produce a rosette of pale-brown segments around the central growing shoot, each bearing 4 ovules at the inner end that develop into the fruit.

Fruits Globular, 2-4 cm long, shiny, yellowish-green turning brown, covered with a bluish powder. They are borne in clusters of usually 4, and contain a single ovate seed, which can be eaten after soaking out the toxins. Fruiting from March to September.

Habitat Widespread and locally common, growing in sunny sites in open forests and woodlands, usually on hillsides on sandy soil. They often form scattered colonies in areas where forest fires are common, and regenerate quickly after fire. The seed takes 6-18 months to germinate, and the seedlings are very slow growing. Advanced specimens transplant easily.

Distribution Tropical inland areas of the NT, northeastern WA and northeastern Qld.

Family Cycadaceae.

Cycas media

Zamia Palm

The Zamia Palm is a medium-sized, stout, palm-like cycad found in the open forests of tropical northern and eastern Australia. This distinctive plant has an erect to spreading crown of leathery, dark-green leaves emerging from the top of a thick and often fire-blackened trunk. Spectacular flushes of erect, bright yellowish-green new leaves are produced after fire.

Trunk Grey to black, to 4 m tall and 35 cm diameter, usually unbranched, although it may occasionally fork in the lower part. It is woody outside and noticeably patterned with closely-packed triangular leaf scars.

Leaves Stiff and leathery, shiny dark-green above, dull and paler below, and pinnately divided into some 300 closely-spaced, opposite, forward-pointing leaflets. The whole leaf may be up to 2.5 m long and 50 cm across, including the cylindrical leaf stalk which is up to 35 cm long and armed with regularly-spaced yellow spines along the margins. The leaflets are linear to sickle-shaped with short, sharply-pointed tips, 10-20 cm long and 7-10 mm wide, becoming smaller towards the base of the leaf. They have a prominent yellow midvein, depressed above and raised on the undersurface of the leaflet, causing the margins to curl slightly under. Young leaves are bright yellowish-green and may be covered with downy hairs.

Cones Unisexual, borne singly in the centre of the crown on separate male and female plants. The male cone is ovoid, yellowish-brown, downy outside, 12-25 cm long, with many tightly-packed, spirally-arranged, hard, scale-like segments. These are wedge-shaped with a small point on the out-side, with hundreds of tiny pollen-bearing capsules on the undersurface. The cones open when mature to release large amounts of wind-borne pollen. The female cones are globular, about 25 cm across, and open early to produce a rosette of green to pale-brown, leaf-like segments on long stalks around the growing central shoot. The female segments have a large, flattened, triangular apex with serrated margins, tapering to a long, narrow tip. They bear 2-8 ovules along the margins of their green, scurfy stalks, which usually droop under the weight of the maturing fruit that encir-cles the top of the trunk.

Fruits Green turning yellow to orange when ripe, globular, 2-4 cm across. They are borne in clus-ters of 2-8, and contain a single, large, ovate seed with a wrinkled coat surrounded by a fleshy layer about 3 mm thick.

Habitat Open forests and rocky sites, and occasionally rainforests. They are very slow growing, hardy and adaptable to most situations, requiring well-drained soil. The seeds are slow to germi-nate, and may take up to 12 months. Large specimens can be successfully transplanted.

Distribution Widespread and locally common in northern Australia from the NT to eastern Qld as far south as Rockhampton.

Family Cycadaceae.

Lepidozamia peroffskyana

Pineapple Palm

The Pineapple Palm is a medium-sized, stout, palm-like cycad found in wet sclerophyll forests in hilly country of subtropical eastern Australia. This striking and unusual plant has a widely-spreading crown of thick and stiff, spirally-arranged, shiny, dark-green fronds growing from the top of a stout trunk, which bears a very large pineapple-like fruiting cone in the centre.

Trunk Smooth, woody and erect, to 7 m tall and 50 cm diameter. It is light to dark-brown, often blackened by fire, patterned with closely-packed, ovate to diamond-shaped leaf scars. The trunk grows from the top and develops a new, bright-green crown every year or two.

Leaves Light-green and sub-erect when young, becoming shiny dark-green and widely-spreading. They are pinnately divided into more than 200 sickle-shaped leaflets. The whole leaf is 1.5-3 m long, including the smooth, dark-green green stalk which is 30-60 cm long and about 2 cm wide, convex below and ridged along the sides. The leaf stalk has a swollen base covered with short downy hair. The leaflets are stiff and leathery without visible veins, 10-32 cm long and 6-15 mm wide, the lower ones are slightly shorter, but never spine-like. They are slightly contracted at the base, closely-spaced and attached along the central groove along the upper surface of the midrib of the leaf. Velvety rudimentary leaves are crowded around the base of the fruiting cone.

Cones Unisexual, usually solitary, and borne on separate male and female plants. Both are green turning brown, usually stalkless, with many tightly-packed, spirally-arranged, scale-like segments. The male cone is 25-60 cm long and 10-40 cm diameter, somewhat cylindrical and usually twisted and contorted. The segments are 6-8 cm long and 2-3 cm wide, with a pointed, upturned outer tip and a long, inner, fertile section bearing hundreds of pale-brown, pollen-bearing capsules about 1 mm across. The female cones are somewhat conical, 45-80 cm long and 20-30 cm diameter at the base. The segments are 5-8 cm long and 3-7 cm wide, fairly thick and fleshy with a blunt, upturned outer tip and an expanded, flattened, inner part bearing 2 stalkless ovules. The male cones open first, releasing large amounts of wind-borne pollen, some of which adheres to a sticky secretion on the outer surface of the scales of the tightly-closed female cone. The female cones open some weeks later when the fruits are fully formed.

Fruits Reddish-brown to bright-red when ripe, ovoid with small pointed tips, 5-6 cm long and 30-35 mm wide, attached in pairs to the inside of the female cone segments. They have a fleshy outer layer surrounding an ovate seed with a hard woody coat.

Habitat Wet sclerophyll forests and rainforest margins in hilly country, forming small colonies. They grow only about 2 m in 100 years, and regenerate quickly after fire with new bright green fronds arising from the blackened trunk. The seeds take up to one year to germinate.

Distribution Scattered in southeastern Qld and northeastern NSW.

Family Zamiaceae.

Macrozamia communis

Burrawang

The Burrawang is a low cycad, often with a subterranean trunk, found in dry forests along the coast of temperate eastern Australia. This palm-like plant has a spreading crown of 20-100 dull, dark-green, rigid, spiny leaves emerging from the top of the trunk, and bears several large pineapple-like fruiting cones in the centre of the crown every 2 years or more.

Trunk Subterranean in deep soils due to the action of its contractile roots. In shallow soils it grows to 1-2 m tall and 30-60 cm diameter, dark-brown, fibrous and covered with closely-packed, flaky leaf scars.

Leaves Dull dark-green above and slightly paler below with a woolly, swollen base; pinnately divided into 50-130 stiff and rigid, sharply-pointed linear leaflets. The whole leaf is 0.7-3 m long, including the spineless, rigid leaf stalk which is 12-60 cm long and 8-18 mm wide, convex below and flattened above with sharp margins and 2 narrow grooves that extend along the midrib of the leaf. The longest leaflets are 16-40 cm long and 4-12 mm wide, becoming much smaller and widely-spaced towards the base. They are forward-pointing in a horizontal plane on either side of the midrib of the leaf, and have a slightly swollen, yellowish base. The upper ones are crowded and the lower ones 3-6 cm apart and spine-like. Young leaves are folded with the tips of their leaflets together. The leaflets have 7-13 scarcely raised parallel veins visible on the under surface.

Cones Borne on separate male and female plants, with 1-10 cones per plant. Both sexes are green turning brown, cylindrical with pointed ends, 20-50 cm long and 8-20 cm across with stalks 8-30 cm long and 2-4 cm thick, arising from the leaf bases within the crown. They have many tightly-packed, spirally-arranged, scale-like segments, bearing long, upward-pointing, flattened green spines, 4-10 cm long in females and 2-5 cm long in males. Male cone segments are 2-4 cm long and wide, broadly obovate to heart-shaped, brown to yellow on the flattened inner side, and covered below with hundreds of pale-brown, pollen-bearing capsules about 1 mm across. Female cone segments are 4-7 cm long and 8-14 cm wide, salmon-pink on the fairly thick and fleshy inner side, which bears 2 stalkless ovules. At maturity the female segments fall away from the cone with the fruits attached, and ripen slowly on the ground. The male cones open first, releasing large amounts of wind-borne pollen.

Fruits Orange to scarlet, ovoid with small pointed tips, 3-5 cm long and 2-3 cm wide, attached in pairs to the inside of the female cone segments. They have a fleshy outer layer surrounding an ovate seed with a hard woody coat.

Habitat Dry sclerophyll forests on deep or shallow sandy or stony soils, often forming dense stands. They are slow growing and will regenerate after fire.

Distribution Abundant in many parts of the coast and adjacent ranges of NSW from the Macleay River on the central north coast, south to Bega on the far south coast, and inland as far as the head of the Goulburn River.

Family Zamiaceae.

Macrozamia moorei

This palm-like plant is a medium-sized cycad with a stout trunk, and is found in open forests along the coast of subtropical eastern Australia. It has a spreading crown of up to 150 dull, bluish-green, rigid, spiny leaves emerging from the top of the trunk, and bears several large pineapple-like fruiting cones in the centre of the crown every 2 years or more.

Trunk Thick and bulbous, 2-7 m tall and 30-80 cm diameter, dark-grey and covered with small, triangular to ovoid, closely-packed leaf scars. Epiphytic plants are sometimes found growing on the trunk.

Leaves Dull bluish-green to greyish-green, pinnately divided into 100-250 stiff and rigid, sharply-pointed linear leaflets. The whole leaf is 1.5-3 m long, including the short, spineless, rigid leaf stalk, which is 5-10 cm long and 2-3 cm wide, flattened above and ridged below, with a bulbous base. The longest leaflets are 20-40 cm long and 5-11 mm wide, becoming gradually smaller towards the base, the lower pairs are almost spine-like and very small. They are forward-pointing and emerge in a horizontal plane or at a slight upward angle on either side of the midrib of the leaf. The bases of the leaflets are narrowed with a yellowish swelling at the attachment point. The upper leaflets are crowded and the lower ones 1-3 cm apart. Young leaves are folded with the tips of the leaflets together. The leaflets have 7-12 scarcely raised parallel veins visible on the under surface.

Cones Borne on separate male and female plants, with 1-8 females and usually 15-100 male cones per plant. Both are greyish-green or bluish-green, cylindrical with pointed ends and short, thick stalks. They arise from the leaf bases within the crown and have many tightly-packed, spirally-arranged, scale-like segments bearing long, upward-pointing, flattened green spines to 7 cm long in females and 2 cm long in males. The male cones are 30-45 cm long and 6-10 cm diameter, often curved when older. Their segments are 2-3 cm long and 15-20 mm wide, broadly obovate, brown to yellow on the flattened inner side, and covered below with hundreds of pale-brown, pollen-bearing capsules about 1 mm across. The female cones are 40-90 cm long and 12-25 cm diameter with a stalk 15-20 cm long and about 3 cm across. Their segments are 5-7 cm long and 4-8 cm wide, salmon-pink on their fairly thick and fleshy inner side, which bears 2 stalkless ovules. At maturity the female segments fall away from the cone with the fruits attached, and ripen slowly on the ground. The male cones open first, releasing large amounts of wind-borne pollen.

Fruits Orange to scarlet, ovoid with indented sides, 4-6 cm long and 2-3 cm wide, attached in pairs to the inside of the female cone segments. They have a fleshy outer layer surrounding an ovate seed with a hard woody coat.

Habitat Wet sclerophyll forests and rainforest margins, generally on steep slopes. They are very slow growing, reaching 2 m in 100 years. They will grow in dry conditions and regenerate successfully after fire.

Distribution Locally abundant in parts of the coast and adjacent ranges of northern NSW from the Clarence River north to Rockhampton in Qld.

Family Zamiaceae.

Musa banksii

Native Banana

The Native Banana is a tall, tree-like, clumping banana found in the tropical rainforests of north-eastern Australia, New Guinea and Samoa. This herbaceous plant has a fleshy stem with clear sap, giving rise to 7-8 spirally-arranged long, wide, glossy-green leaves. Dead leaves usually hang from the crown and a number of suckers are usually present at the base.

Stem Light-green with light-brown and purplish-brown areas, to 6 m tall and about 15 cm diameter. The stem is soft, fleshy and is composed of tightly-wrapped long, sheathing leaf bases, and retains the papery, brown remains of the old leaves for some time. The main stem dies after fruiting and is replaced by one or more basal suckers.

Leaves Shiny dark-green above and paler below, oblong to ovate, usually 1.2-2.5 m long and 50-80 cm wide. The leaves have a stout, green to purplish-brown stalk, 50-80 cm long and about 25 mm diameter, deeply-channelled above and convex below, and expanding at the base to completely encircle the stem. The leaf blade has a pale-green midrib, deeply-channelled above and prominently raised below. Parallel lateral veins spaced about 1 cm apart cross the leaf blade at right angles to the midrib, forming slight ridges along the surface of the leaf. The leaves are easily shredded by the wind.

Inflorescence A drooping raceme with a thick stalk more than 1 m long emerging from the top of the stem. The flowers are arranged along the stalk in transverse clusters (hands) of 10-20. Each hand is located at the base of a large yellowish-green bract about 10 cm long that falls away before the fruits grow. The bracts are closely wrapped in spirals around the stalk, forming a terminal, hard, pointed, ovoid bud. Each bract and its flowers open together; the bract curling back to reveal the flowers. This procedure continues down the stalk, the fruits ripen along the upper part as the bracts unfold from the bud at the tip of the stalk.

Flowers Male, female or bisexual, and produced on the same inflorescence. They are creamy-yellow, striped, tubular, split to the base on one side, 27-45 mm long and 8-12 mm wide with 4 teeth at the tip. The upper flowers are usually male with 5 stamens and a similar-sized style. The lower flowers are usually female, with narrower segments and a club-shaped style and a lobed stigma above a 3-celled ovary with numerous ovules.

Fruits Green turning yellow when ripe, cylindrical, straight or curved, 8-14 cm long and 15-23 mm diameter. They are produced in bunches of 12-20 along the inflorescence, each with a stalk 15-60 mm long, and are packed with many small angular seeds 4-5 mm across embedded in a pithy substance.

Habitat Usually grows along streams, in tropical rainforest clearings and margins. They reproduce from suckers around the base or from seeds, requiring a moist, well-drained site, and will survive in subtropical regions.

Distribution Northeastern Qld from Iron Range in the Cape York Peninsula to Townsville, also found in New Guinea and Samoa.

Family Musaceae.

Asplenium australasicum
Bird's Nest Fern

A large, tufted fern growing on rocks or trees, with a short, erect rhizome clothed with thin grey or purplish scales, giving rise to a funnel-shaped rosette of fronds that collects water and organic debris to nourish the plant. **Fronds** Pale to dark-green, erect, undivided, usually 60-80 cm long (rarely 2 m) and 3-21 cm wide, broad-linear and tapering to a point. They are leathery with entire, wavy margins. The prominent dark-brown midrib is channelled above with a protruding ridge below. Many fine parallel veins run from the central vein to the margins where they are connected to a continuous marginal vein. **Sporangia** Arranged in numerous narrow linear clusters, 1 mm wide and often 4-6 cm long, extending along the fine parallel veins from near the midrib to part way across the fertile fronds. **Habitat** Grows in rainforests and protected sites in open forests, on rocks and trees, preferring filtered sunlight and drier situations, although they will grow on the ground in well-drained soil. Commonly found in tropical and temperate areas along the coast and adjacent ranges from northeastern Qld through NSW to northeastern Vic. **Family** Aspleniaceae.

Microsorum punctatum

A medium-sized fern, often forming large colonies on rocks, with a medium-creeping, fleshy, green rhizome sparsely covered with brown scales. **Fronds** Pale-green, erect or semi-erect, undivided and fairly closely spaced along the rhizome. They are lanceolate with a rounded tip, 40-120 cm long, leathery and coarse with a prominent pale-brown to green central vein, raised on the upper surface, and distinctly ridged towards the base of the frond. A number of well-spaced thin marginal veins are just visible. **Sporangia** Arranged in tiny, distinct, rounded clusters, about 1.5 mm across and irregularly scattered on the underside of the upper part of the frond. **Habitat** Grows in rainforest margins, open forests and gullies, usually on rocks and boulders forming large colonies in fairly open situations. Commonly found along the coast, nearby ranges and tablelands of Qld. This is a fairly hardy tropical species and will tolerate exposure to full sun, but is very frost tender. **Family** Polypodiaceae.

Microsorum scandens
Fragrant Fern

A small, vigorous, scrambling fern climbing for long distances over rocks and tree trunks, with a very long-creeping, tough and wiry rhizome covered with persistent narrow, brown, papery scales. **Fronds** Dark-green, semi-erect or upright, 20-50 cm long and 20 cm wide, thin, often with a musky fragrance, entire with lobed margins. The fronds are sometimes deeply cut, almost to the midrib, and are often rippled. The midrib is distinctly raised above, and each lobe has a thin, wavy, central vein. **Sporangia** Arranged in distinct circular or ovate clusters, 1-3 mm diameter, sunken into the leaf surface and close to the margins of the underside of the fertile fronds. **Habitat** Grows in rainforests and fern gullies, climbing and trailing over rocks and tree trunks, often forming mats in shady sites in areas of high humidity with access to plenty of water. This species is locally abundant along the coast and adjacent ranges from northeastern Qld through NSW to eastern Vic. and Lord Howe Island. **Family** Polypodiaceae.

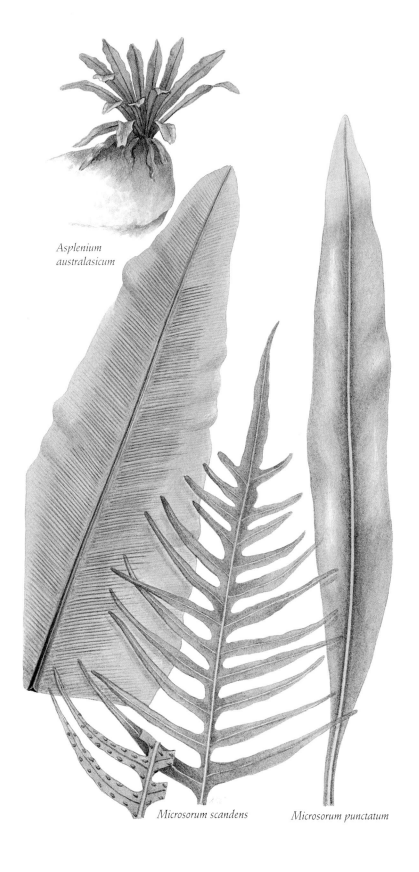

Asplenium australasicum

Microsorum scandens

Microsorum punctatum

Platycerium superbum   **Staghorn Fern**

A large, bracketing epiphytic fern growing on trees and rocks, with a short-creeping, sparsely-branching rhizome with fine rootlets clothed with loose, papery scales and covered by dead leaves. **Fronds** Of two types. Sterile fronds (nest leaves) are produced first. They are light grey-green, up to 60 cm across, hairy when young, becoming smooth. They form a domed lower part, tightly pressed against the host and completely covering the roots, thus protecting the root system from drying winds. The upper part becomes deeply lobed and antler-like, acting as a very efficient trap for falling debris. The nest leaves fold inwards when mature, holding the debris against the root system to create a rich humus that retains water and nourishes the plant. Fertile fronds are spreading to pendant when mature, light grey-green and 0.75-2 m long. Two fertile fronds are produced each year, they are broadly forked into 2 narrow segments which are often twisted and forked a number of times to produce many lobes, 15-40 mm wide. **Sporangia** Produced in large masses to form a brown patch, 10-50 cm diameter, on the underside of the first fork of the fertile fronds. The sporangia are protected by a thick covering of star-like scales attached by fine threads which fall off when mature to release the spores. The terminal lobes of these fronds are sterile. **Habitat** This species is a protected plant. It grows mainly in rainforests on tree trunks and branches, and sometimes on damp rocks and boulders. It is hardy and locally common along the coast and tablelands of Qld and northern NSW as far south as Nabiac, and commonly cultivated as far south as Melbourne. It does not produce small plantlets. **Family** Polypodiaceae.

Platycerium bifurcatum   **Elkhorn Fern**

A large, bracketing epiphytic fern growing mainly on tree trunks, with a short-creeping, much-branched rhizome with many fine roots, clothed in broad, ribbed scales and covered by dead leaves. **Fronds** Of two types. Sterile fronds (nest leaves) are pale-green, becoming brown and papery with age. They are stalkless, spongy near the centre and thin around the edges, roughly circular or kidney-shaped, convex, 10-30 cm diameter with lobed margins, more deeply cut on the upper edge. The nest leaves collect debris and are replaced each year by new leaves that press the old ones against the rhizome, creating a rich humus that retains water and nourishes the plant. The roots grow into this humus and are protected from drying winds. Fertile fronds are leathery, semi-erect becoming pendulous, pale-green, 25-100 cm long, narrow wedge-shaped at the base and forking 1-3 times in the upper part which is often divided into lobes up to 30 cm long and 3 cm wide. They are shed when old and replaced by new fronds. Both types are covered with star-shaped hairs when young. **Sporangia** Form brown patches covering all or the greater part of the lower surfaces of the lobes of the fertile fronds. Small plants are produced on the outer margins of the nest leaves, continually adding to the size of the clump, allowing it to encircle the tree. The clump sometimes becomes too heavy to be supported by the host. **Habitat** This species is a protected plant. It grows in rainforests and open forests, on tree trunks and branches, and sometimes on damp rocks and boulders. It is very hardy and locally common along the coast and tablelands from northeastern Qld to southern NSW and Lord Howe Is., and is commonly cultivated as far south as Melbourne. **Family** Polypodiaceae.

Platycerium bifurcatum

Platycerium superbum

MW.

Blechnum patersonii   **Strap Water Fern**

A medium-sized, semi-erect, clumping fern with an erect rhizome covered with broad, brown, shiny scales and the bases of the old leaf stalks. **Fronds** Dark-green above and paler below, pink when young, erect to pendant, 20-65 cm long, strap-like, leathery, entire or irregularly lobed (both forms are often produced on the same plant). The margins may have small serrations. The stalk is winged, and the midrib distinctly raised on the underside of the frond. Fertile fronds are usually narrower than the sterile ones, with segments 2-4 mm wide, with a pair of longitudinal veins running parallel to the midrib. Sterile fronds are usually 10-25 mm wide and are broader towards the tip.
Sporangia Arranged in continuous lines on either side of the midrib along the parallel longitudinal veins on the underside of the fertile fronds. **Habitat** Grows in clumps in wet, shady sites in rainforests or in protected areas along creeks and rock crevices in eucalypt forests. This species is commonly found along the coast and tablelands from northeastern Qld through NSW to Vic. and northeastern Tas. **Family** Blechnaceae.

Vittaria elongata   **Tape or Ribbon Fern**

A medium-sized, epiphytic fern growing on rocks and tree trunks, with a short-creeping rhizome to 6 mm diameter, covered with dense, fine, hair-like brown or purplish-black scales. **Fronds** Grow in tufts, dark-green or pale-green, semi-erect or drooping, leathery, narrow-linear and undivided with pointed or rounded tips. Sterile fronds are 4-14 cm long and 1-3 mm wide. Fertile fronds are up to 60 cm long and 3-6 mm wide. They have very oblique veins, sometimes parallel to the sunken midrib. **Sporangia** Arranged in two continuous bands close to and parallel to the margins of the fertile leaves. They extend from the tip about half way along the leaf, and are sunken in the leaf blade. **Habitat** A fairly hardy, common and widespread species, forming attractive pendant clumps in tropical and subtropical rainforests along the coast and tablelands from northeastern Qld to cental eastern NSW as far south as the Watagan Mts. **Family** Vittariaceae.

Pyrrosia rupestris   **Rock Felt Fern**

A small, epiphytic fern growing on trees and rocks, with a long-creeping, much-branched rhizome clothed with pale reddish-brown papery scales. **Fronds** Thick, fleshy and covered with white or reddish star-shaped hairs. Fertile fronds are narrow-lanceolate with entire margins, 4-15 cm long and 3-7 mm wide, whitish below and tapering to a thick stalk. Sterile fronds are spathulate to spoon-shaped or orbicular with entire margins, 1-8 cm long. They both have a prominent midrib and obscure lateral veins. **Sporangia** Arranged in globular clusters, 1-2.5 mm diameter, irregularly situated but densely crowded in 1-4 rows on either side of the midrib on the underside of the fertile fronds, occurring over most of the frond. They sometimes join together with age. **Habitat** Grows in rainforests or wet sites in sclerophyll forests, on tree trunks and rock faces, particularly among clumps of large epiphytes. This hardy species is widespread and common along the coast, tablelands and inland slopes from northeastern Qld through NSW to eastern Vic. **Family** Polypodiaceae.

Blechnum patersonii

Vittaria elongata

Pyrrosia rupestris

MW.

Lindsaea linearis **Screw Fern**

A small, delicate fern with a short-creeping rhizome clothed with narrow, golden-brown scales, giving rise to a rosette-like cluster of fronds. **Fronds** Pale-green, erect or spreading, pinnately divided into stalkless triangular segments. Sterile fronds are shorter than the fertile fronds, 10-30 cm long and usually 8-14 mm wide. Fertile fronds are usually 15-40 cm long and 4-9 mm wide. They are obliquely arranged along the stalk and bent downwards to resemble the thread of a screw. The stalks are thin, wiry and shiny, dark reddish-brown or black. The segments have a number of forked veins fanning out from the base to the uneven, shallowly-lobed outer margins. **Sporangia** Arranged in elongated clusters along the outer margins of the fertile leaf segments. **Habitat** Grows in dry sclerophyll forests, heaths and scrubs, near swamps and in damp, shady depressions on sandy soil, often among rocks, sometimes forming extensive colonies. Widespread and common along the coast and ranges in southeastern Qld, NSW, Vic., southeastern SA, southwestern WA, Tas and Norfolk Island. **Family** Lindsaeaceae.

Pellaea falcata **Sickle Fern**

A medium-sized, hardy fern with a short to medium-creeping, wiry, rigid rhizome, densely clothed with narrow scales. **Fronds** Mostly crowded, erect or semi-erect, dark, shiny-green above and paler below, 12-65 cm long, linear-oblong in outline, pinnately divided into 29-89 alternate or opposite, leathery, ovate to lanceolate or sickle-shaped segments. The segments are 5-60 mm long and 2-15 mm wide with inconspicuous veins and very short stalks to 1 mm long. They are attached to a rigid, glossy, dark-brown stem covered with hair-like scales and ridged above. The young developing fronds are not rolled up as in most ferns, but are folded over like a shepherd's crook. **Sporangia** Arranged in continuous linear clusters about 1 mm wide along the margins of the underside of the fertile leaf segments. **Habitat** Grows in damp, rocky sites in open forests and rainforests, often forming large colonies, along the coast and tablelands of Qld, NSW, Vic., northeastern Tas. and Lord Howe Is. **Family** Sinopteridaceae.

Marsilea drummondii **Common Nardoo**

A small to medium-sized fern growing in water or swamps, with clover-like leaflets borne in groups on long stalks along a long-creeping, much-branched rhizome which is covered with orange-brown hairs. **Fronds** Are 2-30 cm long and comprise very slender stalks bearing two pairs of opposite, sterile leaflets at the end. In aquatic sites the sterile leaflets float on the surface of the water. They are silvery-green, broad wedge-shaped to rounded-triangular, 5-30 mm wide, sometimes with slightly indented margins, hairy when young, becoming smooth in aquatic plants. The veins are fine and numerous, radiating from the base of the leaflets and joined at their ends to form loops. **Sporangia** Contained in solitary, hard, woody, globular cases (sporocarps) formed by modified leaves, 4-9 mm long, attached to the rhizome by unbranched stalks 8-90 mm long. They are produced when the plants are in drier situations. **Habitat** Common in arid areas where it grows in areas subject to intermittent flooding, in depressions and swamps. Found on the inland slopes and plains throughout mainland Australia. **Family** Marsileaceae.

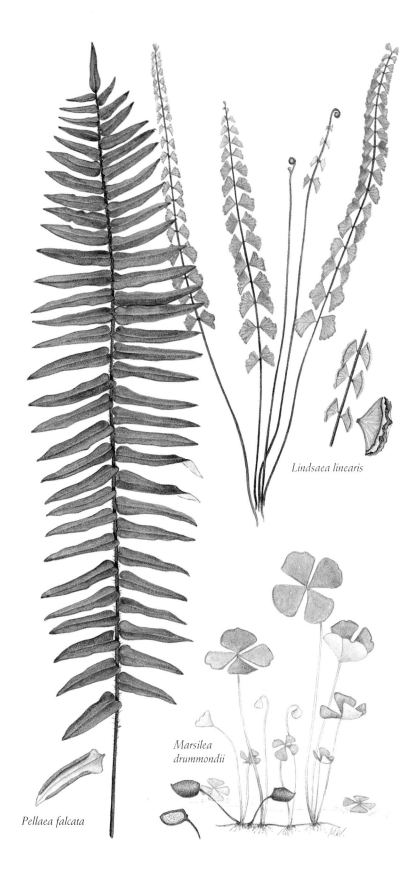

Lindsaea linearis

Marsilea
drummondii

Pellaea falcata

Blechnum nudum
Fishbone Water Fern

A medium to tall fern forming rosette-like clumps, with a short-creeping or erect rhizome, sometimes forming a black fibrous trunk to 1 m tall in older specimens (particularly in rocky sites) with dark, shiny scales near the base. **Fronds** Clustered, erect, 25-60 cm long, sometimes up to 120 cm long, broad lanceolate in outline and dissected down to the midrib into numerous linear segments, giving the frond a pinnate appearance. The segments are dark-green above and paler below, and attached by their broad bases to the glossy, reddish-brown to pale-brown, grooved midrib. They are thin with entire margins, a prominent central vein and forked parallel lateral veins. Fertile fronds arise from the centre of the plant, they are shorter than the sterile ones with narrower segments, 1-3 cm long and 2-3 mm wide. Sterile fronds have the longest segments in the middle, they are 35-120 mm long. **Sporangia** Arranged in continuous linear clusters on either side of the midvein of the fertile fronds. The leaf margins are rolled over giving the fertile segments a compact, rod-like appearance. **Habitat** Grows in a variety of habitats, in rainforests, along creek banks, swamps, tall eucalypt forests, and in many soil types, often forming extensive colonies. This hardy species is common and widespread along the coast and tablelands from northeastern Qld to NSW, Vic., southeastern SA and Tas. **Family** Blechnaceae.

Sticherus lobatus
Spreading Fan Fern

A medium-sized to tall, erect or straggling fern with umbrella-like fronds forming 1-3 tiers, with dormant leaf buds in the forks, and a long-creeping, wiry rhizome covered with brown scales. **Fronds** Are 0.5-2 m long, dull dark-green above and paler below with a long stalk, branching to form 1-3 umbrella-like tiers of spreading, pinnately divided leaves with many narrow, stalkless segments. The leaf segments are crowded, at right angles to the midrib, 10-45 mm long, oblong to linear with pointed tips and entire margins, although the segments at the base of the forks are lobed. They are joined to the midrib by their wide bases. **Sporangia** Arranged in small round clusters on the underside of the fertile leaf segments, forming a single row on each side of the midvein. **Habitat** Grows in rainforest margins and moist areas in tall forests, often forming large colonies on creek banks. This is a fairly widespread and locally common species extending along the coast and tablelands from southeastern Qld through NSW to southwestern Vic. and Tas. **Family** Gleicheniaceae.

Blechnum wattsii
Hard Water Fern

A medium-sized fern forming small, compact clumps, with a medium to long-creeping, much-branched, thick rhizome with dark-brown to black scales with a pale border and finely-toothed margin. **Fronds** Not clustered, erect or semi-erect, 30-70 cm long, occasionally to 120 cm long, with long stalks bearing brown scales, pinnately divided into numerous broad linear to sickle-shaped segments with very short stalks. The segments have slightly irregular, minutely-serrated margins. New fronds are bronze-pink, older fronds are dark-green above and paler below, leathery, the same size or slightly larger at the base of the frond, with blunt tips, a prominent central vein and deeply etched, mostly unforked lateral veins. Sterile fronds have segments up to 18 cm long and 20 mm wide. Fertile fronds are slightly shorter with linear segments, 2-5 mm wide with a pair of parallel longitudinal veins alongside the central vein. **Sporangia** Arranged in continuous linear clusters along the two longitudinal veins of the fertile leaf segments. **Habitat** Grows in large colonies in wet, exposed areas, and occasionally on the trunks of tree ferns, forming the main ground cover in moist, dark sites in rainforests and along creek banks. Common and widespread along the coast and tablelands from southeastern Qld to NSW, Vic., southeastern SA and Tas. **Family** Blechnaceae.

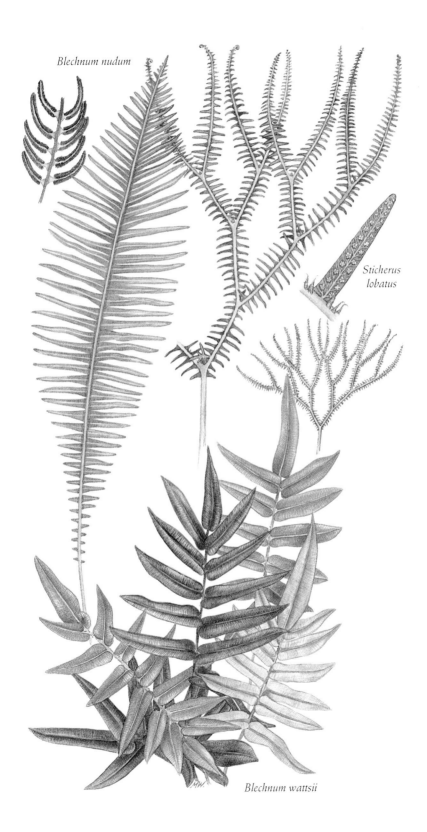

Blechnum nudum

Sticherus lobatus

Blechnum wattsii

Blechnum cartilagineum   **Gristle Fern**

A medium-sized to tall fern forming rosette-like clumps, with a short-creeping rhizome or a short, thick, black trunk densely covered with the bases of the old leaf stalks and narrow black scales. **Fronds** Erect or semi-erect, clustered, pale to dark-green with rosy pink new growth, 50-150 cm long, broadly triangular in outline and dissected down to the midrib into numerous linear to lance-olate pointed segments to give the frond a pinnate appearance. The segments have minutely-ser-rated or entire margins and are attached by their broad bases to the pale-brown midrib which is grooved above and convex below. They are leathery with a prominent central vein and many tiny, forked or simple lateral veins. Sterile fronds have segments 10-15 cm long and 10-15 mm wide. Fertile fronds have narrower segments, 10-15 cm long and 5-10 mm wide, with a pair of longitudinal veins parallel to the central vein. **Sporangia** Arranged in continuous raised linear clusters on each side of the central vein of the fertile leaf segments. **Habitat** Grows in dark, moist areas in rain-forests and tall eucalypt forests, or on rocky sites on hillsides, often forming large colonies. This hardy species is widespread and commonly found along the coast and tablelands from northeast-ern Qld through NSW to Vic., SA and Tas. **Family** Blechnaceae.

Blechnum indicum   **Swamp Water Fern**

A medium-sized to tall, clumping fern with an erect rhizome giving rise to a crown of fronds. **Fronds** Stiff and erect, shiny green, to 110 cm long, pinnately divided into numerous linear to lanceolate segments with short stalks and finely toothed margins. The segments of the upper part of the frond are often stalkless, and the final ones are joined to form a tail. The segments are stiff and leathery, sterile ones are 5-13 cm long and 8-12 mm wide, fertile ones 4-9 cm long and 4-8 mm wide. They have a prominent central vein which is flanked by 2 parallel veins in fertile segments, and small, simple or forked lateral veins. **Sporangia** Arranged in continuous, raised linear clus-ters on each side of the central vein of the fertile leaf segments, usually covering the central vein when mature. **Habitat** Grows in large colonies around the margins of swamps and lakes, often in exposed areas, and resents complete shade. This species is frost-hardy and abundant in the NT, northeastern WA, and from northeastern Qld to central NSW as far south as Jervis Bay. **Family** Blechnaceae.

Sticherus flabellatus   **Umbrella Fern or Shiny Fan Fern**

A medium-sized to tall, clumping fern with umbrella-like fronds and a long-creeping, wiry rhizome covered with brown scales. **Fronds** Are 50-150 cm long, shiny dark-green above and paler below with a long stalk, branching to form umbrella-like tiers of spreading, pinnately divided leaves with many narrow segments. The leaf segments are crowded, forward-pointing, 2-3 cm long and 1-3 mm wide, oblong to linear with pointed tips and serrated margins, joined to the midrib by their wide bases. **Sporangia** Arranged in small round clusters on the underside of the fertile leaf seg-ments, forming a row on each side of the midvein. **Habitat** Grows in rainforest margins and moist areas in tall forests, often forming large colonies on creek banks. This is a fairly widespread and locally common species extending along the coast and tablelands from northeastern Qld through NSW to southeastern Vic. **Family** Gleicheniaceae.

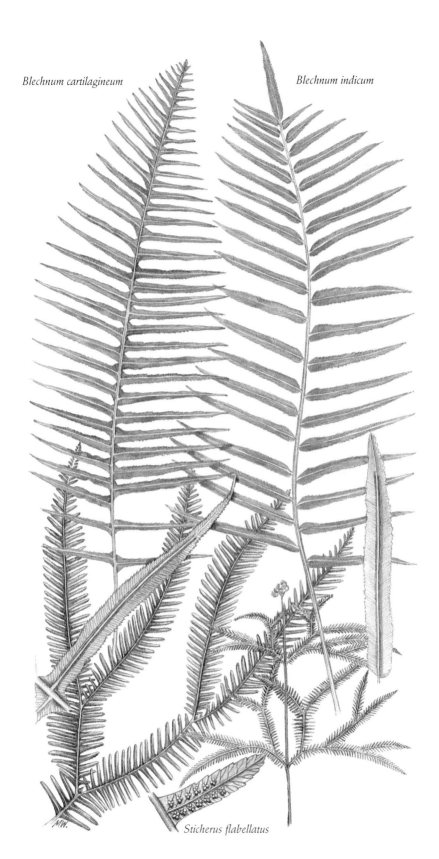

Blechnum cartilagineum

Blechnum indicum

Sticherus flabellatus

Doodia aspera   **Prickly Rasp Fern**

A small, robust, clumping fern with erect fronds arising from a short-creeping rhizome densely covered with narrow black scales and producing long underground suckers to form a spreading, tufted clump. **Fronds** Erect, 10-45 cm long, broad lanceolate in outline and dissected down to the midrib into numerous linear to triangular segments to 6 cm long, giving the frond a pinnate appearance. The pale-green segments are attached by their broad bases to a cream-coloured midrib which is grooved above and convex below; the lowermost pair are sometimes shortly stalked. They are coarse with a prominent central vein and prickly toothed margins. New growth is bright pink to reddish. **Sporangia** Arranged in distinct raised round clusters, 1-2 mm across, sometimes joining together with age, produced in single or double rows along the whole length of the fertile leaf segments on either side of the main vein. **Habitat** Grows in large colonies in tall open eucalypt forests, rainforest gullies and among rocks and boulders in woodlands. This very hardy species is widespread along the coast and tablelands from northeastern Qld through NSW to eastern Vic. **Family** Blechnaceae.

Doodia caudata   **Small Rasp Fern**

A small, robust, clumping fern with semi-erect or pendant fronds arising from a short-creeping rhizome covered with small dark scales and producing underground suckers to form discreet clumps. **Fronds** Almost erect to horizontal with upturned tips, 10-30 cm long, narrow lanceolate in outline and dissected down to the midrib into numerous linear segments to give the frond a pinnate appearance. The dark-green segments are attached by their broad bases to a cream-coloured, grooved midrib; the upper segments are united and the lower segments are attached by short stalks. They are coarse with a prominent central vein and prickly, toothed margins. New growth is often red or pink. The fertile fronds are sometimes narrower, longer and more erect. **Sporangia** Arranged in raised round clusters, 1-2 mm long, and may form a continuous strip along the midvein of the fertile leaf segments, sometimes covering the whole under surface in older specimens. **Habitat** Grows in rainforests, forests and woodlands, usually in moist sites and rock crevices, and sometimes on the trunks of living tree ferns. This species is widespread and locally common from northeastern Qld through NSW to Vic, SA, Tas., Lord Howe Is. and Norfolk Is. **Family** Blechnaceae.

Doodia media   **Common Rasp Fern**

A small, robust, clumping fern with erect fronds arising from a short-creeping rhizome densely covered with small, thick, black scales, and producing underground suckers, giving rise to spreading clumps. **Fronds** Erect, 10-60 cm long, narrow-lanceolate in outline and pinnately divided into numerous linear segments. The upper segments are attached by broad bases to a grooved, pale midrib. The majority of the segments have short, rough, black stalks, and the terminal ones are united. The segments are dark-green, rough with a prominent central vein and finely-serrated, prickly margins. New growth is pink to red. **Sporangia** Oblong, about 1 mm long, arranged in raised rows on either side of the central vein of the fertile leaf segments, eventually covering the whole under surface. **Habitat** Grows in small colonies in rainforests, open forests and gullies in shady or exposed sites, particularly in rocky crevices. This is a hardy species growing from northeastern Qld through eastern NSW to Vic. and northeastern Tas. **Family** Blechnaceae.

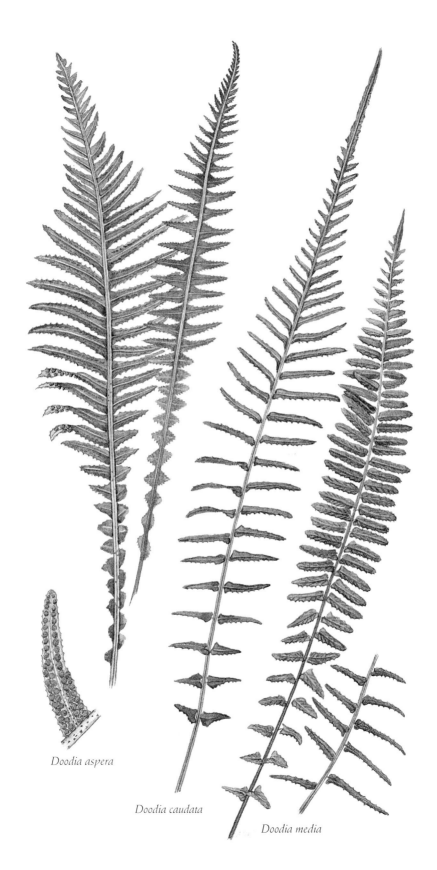

Doodia aspera

Doodia caudata

Doodia media

Nephrolepis cordifolia   **Fishbone Fern**

A medium-sized to tall, tufted fern with a short, erect rhizome covered with shiny brown scales, with long, wiry runners that produce fleshy bulbs. **Fronds** Erect or pendant, dull pale-green, to 1 m long, pinnately divided into numerous narrow-linear to sickle-shaped segments with rounded tips and very short stalks or stalkless. The segments are 15-60 mm long and 4-9 mm wide with small irregular teeth on the margins, and often overlap. The leaf stalk and midrib are shiny brown, ridged above, with hair-like scales. The segments have a distinct central vein and indistinct parallel marginal veins. **Sporangia** Arranged in raised brown kidney-shaped clusters about 1 mm across, in two rows close to the margins on the underside of the fertile leaf segments. **Habitat** Grows on the ground in rocky sites, or as an epiphyte among the leaf bases of palms, in rainforests, open forests and in wet rocky clefts. This is a very hardy and adaptable fern, tolerating shade and full sun, growing along the coast and tablelands of eastern Qld, northeastern NSW and central NT. **Family** Davalliaceae.

Callipteris prolifera

A large fern with a large rosette of fleshy fronds arising from an erect rhizome clothed with dark-brown to black, minutely-toothed scales, that may form a short trunk in old plants. **Fronds** Pale to dark-green, 0.5-2 m tall, pinnately divided into large, fleshy, pointed, lanceolate segments, 15-30 cm long and 25-40 mm wide with shallow teeth along the margins. Much smaller accessory segments with entire margins are produced at the base of the larger segments. The fronds bear numerous fleshy plantlets along the midrib, and these grow independently when the main frond dies. The main stalks are stout and covered with rough projections. Small veins run from the midveins to the teeth along the margins of the segments. **Sporangia** Arranged in linear clusters along the smaller veins to form V-shaped pairs on the underside of the fertile leaf segments. **Habitat** Grows in shady sites in lowland tropical rainforests and needs an abundance of water. It is locally common in northeastern Qld. **Family** Athyriaceae.

Adiantum diaphanum   **Filmy Maidenhair Fern**

A small, delicate fern with a branched, short-creeping, tufted rhizome clothed with dark reddish-brown narrow scales, with prominent buds on the roots. **Fronds** Dark-green, 10-35 cm long with slender black stalks, mostly pinnately divided into membranous, oblong to ovate segments with short stalks and toothed outer margins. The lower part of the frond may be forked again to give that part a bipinnate appearance. The segments are 3-15 mm long and 3-12 mm wide with minute, stiff, dark hairs near the margins, and a few free veins. **Sporangia** Arranged in small, globular clusters in deep notches between the teeth along the margins of the fertile leaf segments. There are usually 3-8 clusters per segment. **Habitat** Grows in wet, shady sites, often on dripping rock faces and earth banks, near waterfalls and streams, forming extensive colonies, usually in rainforests. This is a widespread species found along the coast and tablelands from northeastern Qld through NSW to southeastern Vic. **Family** Adiantaceae.

*Nephrolepis
cordifolia*

*Callipteris
prolifera*

Adiantum diaphanum

MW.

Asplenium polyodon (syn. *A. falcatum*) **Sickle Spleenwort**

A small to large epiphytic fern growing on trees or rocks, with a medium-creeping thick rhizome densely covered with brown scales. This is a very variable species forming arching or pendulous clumps, and may occasionally produce new plants from buds on the fronds. **Fronds** Dark-green, semi-erect or pendant, thin, 25-150 cm long, narrowly-triangular in outline, usually pinnately divided into lobed or toothed, tapering, slightly sickle-shaped segments, the lower ones may be again divided, and the upper segments are joined to form a long tail. The leaf segments are stiff and range in size from 3-15 cm long, with a central vein giving rise to a number of forked side veins. The midrib of the frond is blackish-purple below with a green ridge above, joined to the segments by short stalks. **Sporangia** Arranged in distinct, raised, strap-like clusters, 7-11 mm long, following the secondary veins of the fertile leaf segments. **Habitat** Grows in tropical and temperate rain-forests where it forms large clumps of hanging fronds on trees and rocks in coarse, well-drained soil, and is often found growing from the base of other epiphytes. This is a very slow-growing but hardy species, preferring shady, humid conditions. It is found along the coast and adjacent ranges from northeastern Qld through NSW to eastern Vic. **Family** Aspleniaceae.

Schellolepis subauriculata

A medium-sized, erect or pendulous, epiphytic fern, often growing among the roots of other epiphytes, with a medium-creeping fleshy rhizome, scaly when young, but becoming smooth and white when older. **Fronds** Erect, becoming pendulous when older, pale-green, to 1 m long, pinnately divided into well-spaced lanceolate segments with toothed margins. The segments are stalkless, thin, with a prominent central vein and inconspicuous, branched lateral veins, often with two ear-like lobes at the base. The main stalk is pale to dark-brown, ridged, with scattered hair-like scales. **Sporangia** Arranged in distinct rounded clusters in shallow depressions on the under-side of the fertile leaf segments, in two rows between the margins and the central vein. **Habitat** Grows in forested areas as an epiphyte among other epiphytic plants such as ferns and orchids, and occasionally on the ground. This species is commonly found along the coast and tablelands of northeastern Qld. **Family** Polypodiaceae.

Drynaria rigidula **Basket Fern**

A large epiphytic fern usually growing on rocks or trees with a large, creeping rhizome covered with conspicuous long, reddish-brown fringed scales. **Fronds** Two kinds of fronds are produced alter-nately along the rhizome, both are covered entirely or in part with narrow, fringed scales and star-shaped hairs. The sterile "nest" fronds are long and narrow, 10-36 cm long and 6-8 cm wide, stalk-less, slightly to deeply lobed, becoming brown and papery. They are entire, erect, and collect falling debris to provide humus for the root system and protect the rhizome from the sun. Fertile fronds are erect or arching, pale-green, 30-150 cm long and pinnately divided into 30-40 linear to lanceo-late segments. They have a long, brown, slightly winged stalk. The leaf segments are leathery with a prominent central vein and a network of tiny secondary veins; their margins have small irregular serrations. **Sporangia** Arranged in distinct raised round clusters forming single rows on either side of the central veins of the fertile leaf segments. **Habitat** Grows on trees or wet rocks, creeping or clump-forming, found in moist forests and rainforests from northeastern Qld to north-eastern NSW as far south as the Clarence River. **Family** Polypodiaceae.

Asplenium polyodon

Schellolepis subauriculata

Drynaria rigidula

MW.

Pteris ensiformis   **Slender Brake**

A small, erect fern with a short-creeping, branching, fleshy rhizome clothed with dark-brown lanceolate scales, producing clumps of fronds. **Fronds** Dark-green, to 35 cm long, pinnately divided into a few long, linear segments with irregularly-toothed margins, some of the lower ones are often lobed or further divided. The leaf segments are 5-16 cm long at the base of the frond, decreasing in size towards the tip, they are stalkless or on very short stalks with a prominent central vein and numerous lateral veins. The main stalk is slender, pale, distinctly grooved, to 20 cm long. Sterile fronds are shorter with irregularly-toothed segments. Fertile fronds have narrower segments toothed only near the tips. **Sporangia** Arranged in continuous linear clusters along the margins of the underside of the fertile leaf segments, protected by the curled-over margins. **Habitat** Grows in rainforest margins and muddy estuarine areas, forming compact clumps, from sea-level to about 500 m along the coast of eastern Qld; naturalized in the Sydney region. **Family** Pteridaceae.

Christella dentata (syn. *Cyclosorus nymphalis*)   **Binung**

A medium-sized, coarse, clumping fern with a rosette of fronds and a short-creeping rhizome that may develop into a short trunk, densely-clothed with narrow brown scales 89-10 mm long and 1 mm wide. **Fronds** Erect or arching, pale to dark-green, 40-100 cm long and 12-18 cm wide, pinnately divided into lobed or toothed, stalkless segments tapering to a fine point; the lowermost pairs are smaller, more distant and often ear-like, 3-5 cm long. The leaf segments are thin and clothed with minute hairs, particularly along the central vein. The main leaf stalk is dark-brown, ridged, and covered with minute grey hairs. **Sporangia** Arranged in distinct raised round clusters on either side of the lateral veins of the fertile leaf segments. **Habitat** Grows in spreading tussocks along creeks or in swamps or other wet areas in rainforest margins and sclerophyll forests. Widespread and common from northeastern Qld to the central coast of NSW, Vic., eastern SA, northern WA, northern NT and Lord Howe Is. This is a very hardy species preferring partial sun and plenty of water. **Family** Thelypteridaceae.

Cyrtomium falcatum   **Holly Fern**

A small, clumping fern with a short-creeping, erect rhizome densely clothed with broad, reddish-brown scales. **Fronds** Shiny dark-green above and paler below, to 60 cm long, broadly-triangular in outline, pinnately divided into 9-15 pairs of broad, holly-like, sickle-shaped segments with sharply-toothed, lobed margins and short stalks. The leaf segments are 6-10 cm long and 2-4 cm wide, leathery, with a prominent central vein and a network of small lateral veins. The main leaf stalk is pale to dark-brown, deeply ridged and densely covered with coarse scales below the segments. **Sporangia** Arranged in distinct raised round clusters scattered over the underside of the fertile leaf segments. **Habitat** Grows in rock crevices, particularly on coastal cliffs well above the high water mark. Native to Japan, it is widely cultivated throughout Australia and has become naturalised in southeastern Qld, the central coast of NSW, northeastern Vic. and southeastern SA. This is an extremely hardy species and will tolerate very exposed positions and temperature extremes. **Family** Dryopteridaceae.

Pteris ensiformis

Christella dentata

Cyrtomium falcatum

Polyphlebium venosum

A small, epiphytic, filmy fern growing on tree fern trunks, with a long-creeping, much-branched rhizome densely clothed with red-brown hairs. **Fronds** Translucent, pale-green, pendant, 3-16 cm long, pinnately divided into 2-9 pairs of variable, irregularly-lobed, oblong to linear segments, stalkless or with very short stalks. They have prominent, branched veins and may have a few small hairs. **Sporangia** Arranged in thread-like clusters 2-3 mm long, growing from the edge of the fertile leaf segments. They are usually solitary, emerging from the margin of one of the lobes near the base of the segment, and are enclosed in a cone-shaped membrane with a bristly tip, 2-15 mm long. **Habitat** Grows in extensive colonies covering the trunks of tree ferns, especially *Dicksonia antarctica*, tree trunks and logs in rainforests, and is commonly found along the coast and tablelands from southeastern Qld through NSW to Vic. and Tas. **Family** Hymenophyllaceae.

Tectaria muelleri

A medium-sized, clumping fern with a short-creeping rhizome covered with pale-brown scales, giving rise to a rosette of erect or semi-erect fronds with fine white hairs on the curled new fronds and bases of the stalks. **Fronds** Pale-green, becoming dark-green with age, thin-textured, broadly triangular in outline, to 80 cm long and 40 cm wide. They are pinnately divided into large, deeply lobed segments. The segments have short stalks at the base of the frond and are attached by their broad bases towards the top. The bottom segments are larger and more deeply lobed and point towards the top of the frond. They have a prominent central vein and tiny, forked marginal veins. **Sporangia** Arranged in distinct, kidney-shaped clusters between the central vein and margins of the underside of the fertile leaf segments. **Habitat** Grows in dense highland rainforests along the coastal ranges and tablelands of northeastern Qld. This is a hardy species, cultivated in shady sites in frost-free areas as far south as southern Vic. **Family** Dryopteridaceae.

Pteris umbrosa

A tall, clumping fern with a short-creeping, thick, freely-branching rhizome clothed with narrow, dark-brown scales. **Fronds** Glossy dark-green, erect or semi-erect, to 2.6 m long on stalks to 1 m long, grooved above. They are pinnately divided into long, stalkless, linear to lanceolate segments with broad bases, the lower ones are stalked and divided again into 3-5 spreading segments. The segments are up to 30 cm long with a prominent central vein and entire or minutely-serrated margins. The sterile segments are slightly broader than the fertile ones. **Sporangia** Arranged in continuous linear strips along the margins of the underside of the fertile leaf segments. **Habitat** Grows in colonies along creek beds, usually among rocks in rainforests along the coast and adjacent ranges from northeastern Qld through NSW to southeastern Vic. A very hardy fern and popular in cultivation. **Family** Pteridaceae.

Polyphlebium venosum

Tectaria muelleri

Pteris umbrosa

Gleichenia dicarpa

Pouched Coral Fern

A tall, scrambling fern forming tangled masses, with a long-creeping, much-branched, slender, wiry rhizome clothed with dark scales. **Fronds** Dull-green, to 2 m long and 9 cm wide, forked several times and bipinnately divided into many tiny, rounded segments attached by their broad bases to the hairy midrib. The segments are 1-1.5 mm long, their margins are curled under to form pouches. The fronds are borne on a long, brown, woolly stalk. **Sporangia** Very small and only visible with a lens, they are pale-yellow and contained in the pouches on the underside of the fertile leaf segments. There are usually two sporangia in one corner of the pouch on each segment. **Habitat** Grows in large colonies along creek beds, cliffs and swamps in rainforest margins, dry sclerophyll forests and scrubs, in wet, sunny sites, usually with the roots in water and the fronds in the sun. This species is common and widespread along the coast and tablelands from northeastern Qld through NSW to Vic. and Tas. **Family** Gleicheniaceae.

Lunathyrium petersenii

A small to medium-sized fern with a short-creeping, fleshy rhizome to 5 m diameter, clothed with light-brown, thinly-pointed scales. This species was previously identified as *Lunathyrium japonicum*, which is confined to Japan. **Fronds** Dark-green above and paler below, erect, 30-80 cm long including a stout stalk to 40 cm long, grooved on the upper surface and darker at the base. They are broadly triangular and pinnately divided towards the top of the fronds into lobed segments with small serrations. The lower parts are usually bipinnately divided, with the segments divided to the midribs. The tiny lateral veins are simple or forked. **Sporangia** Arranged in broadly linear to oblong clusters about 2 mm long on the underside of the fertile leaf segments in rows following the small lateral veins. **Habitat** Grows in colonies along steam banks, rock faces and other damp sites, often in exposed areas in rainforests and wet sclerophyll forests along the coast and tablelands from northeastern Qld to the central coast of NSW. **Family** Athyriaceae.

Gleichenia microphylla

Parasol or Scrambling Coral Fern

A medium-sized to tall, scrambling fern with a long-creeping, slender, wiry rhizome clothed with scales in the younger parts. **Fronds** Fine and delicate, dark-green above and paler below, 1-3 m long, forked several times and bipinnately divided into many tiny, triangular-ovate, flat segments, 1-2 mm long, attached by their broad bases to the hairy midrib. The fronds are borne on a long, brown, smooth or scaly-hairy stalk. **Sporangia** Pale-yellow, very small and only visible with a lens. They are in groups of 2-4, immersed in a slight cavity near the upper basal angle on the underside of the fertile leaf segments. **Habitat** Grows in large, tangled masses on exposed sites on wet soil on sandstone cliffs, swamps, scrubs and dry sclerophyll forests. This species is common and widespread along the coast and tablelands from northeastern Qld through NSW to Vic., southeastern SA and Tas. **Family** Gleicheniaceae.

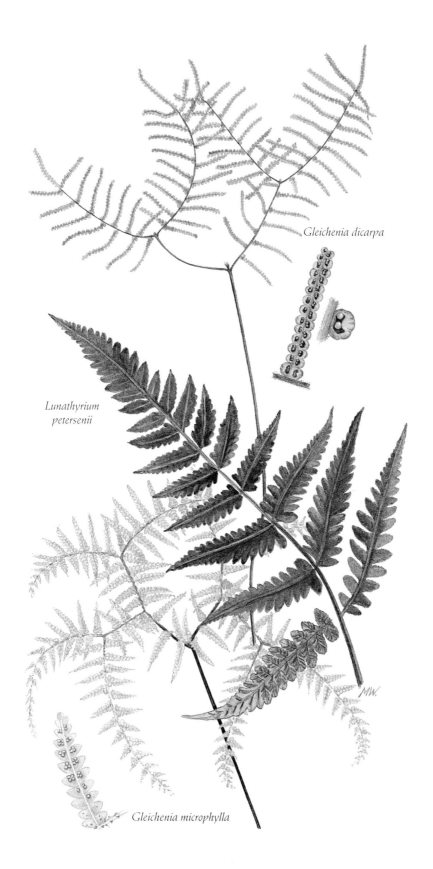

Gleichenia dicarpa

Lunathyrium petersenii

MW.

Gleichenia microphylla

Asplenium bulbiferum   **Mother Spleenwort**

A medium-sized to tall, clumping, terrestrial or epiphytic fern with a short, tufted rhizome clothed with dull brown scales. **Fronds** Dark-green, erect or semi-pendulous, to 1.2 m long, broadly-lanceolate in outline. They have a winged, scaly midrib and are usually bipinnately divided into many lobed segments, the lower ones may be deeply cut to give them a tripinnate appearance, while the upper ones are often only pinnately divided. They are thin-textured with free veins and produce small plantlets towards the tips of some of the segments. These develop slowly and are able to grow alone when the frond dies. **Sporangia** Arranged in oblong to elliptical raised clusters, 2-4 mm long, on the underside of the fertile leaf segments. Each segment has 2-4 clusters positioned at the base of the lobes close to the margins. **Habitat** Grows in scattered colonies in rainforests and fern gullies in cool, humid, shady sites, often growing on the trunks of tree ferns and on rocks. This hardy species is commonly found from southeastern Qld through eastern NSW, Vic. and Tas., and rarely in southeastern SA. **Family** Aspleniaceae.

Pteris pacifica

A medium-sized to tall, clumping fern with a short-creeping, much-branched rhizome. **Fronds** Erect, shiny dark-green, to 1 m tall, broadly triangular in outline, single or divided into 3 parts. The fronds have a shiny brown stalk and are bipinnately divided into many linear segments up to 3 cm long, attached almost at right-angles to the midrib by their broad bases. The segments have prominent forked marginal veins. **Sporangia** Arranged in a raised, broken or continuous band along the margins of the underside of the fertile leaf segments. **Habitat** Grows in large, dense colonies in wet sites in rainforests, rainforest margins and sclerophyll forests. This hardy species is widespread along the coast and tablelands of northeastern Qld. **Family** Pteridaceae.

Pteris tremula   **Tender Brake**

A tall, clumping fern with a thick, short-creeping, erect rhizome clothed with narrow brown scales and bearing multiple crowns of fronds. **Fronds** Pale-green and erect, to 2 m long with a shiny brown stalk grooved on the upper surface. The fronds are bipinnately divided into numerous deeply-lobed segments, some of which may be cut down to the midrib to give the frond a tripinnate appearance. The segments are thin and membranous with a prominent central vein and entire or once-forked marginal veins. The ultimate segments are narrow-oblong to linear, to 2 cm long. Sterile segments have very finely-toothed margins, while the fertile segments have entire margins and are much narrower. **Sporangia** Arranged in a broken or continuous band along the margins of the underside of the fertile leaf segments. **Habitat** Grows in a variety of habitats including rainforests, sclerophyll forests, wet, shaded gullies and gorges. This is a fast-growing species, widespread along the coast, tablelands and inland in all mainland states except WA. **Family** Pteridaceae.

*Asplenium
bulbiferum*

*Pteris
pacifica*

MW.

Pteris tremula

Lastreopsis munita   **Naked Shield Fern**

A small, erect fern with a medium-creeping rhizome, sparsely covered with dark-brown or black scales, giving rise to relatively widely-spaced fronds. **Fronds** Glossy pale-green, 40-90 cm long, broadly triangular in outline and mostly bipinnately divided into many small segments. Some of the lower segments may be divided again, while the terminal segments are undivided. They have sharp teeth on the margins, although the ultimate segments have thickened margins and fewer teeth. The main stalk is ridged with a channel above filled with hairs and continuous with the secondary stalks. The segments have a prominent central vein on the underside, and sparsely-branched marginal veins. **Sporangia** Arranged in distinct, raised, round clusters on the underside of the fertile leaf segments along the marginal veins, usually forming a row on either side of the central vein. **Habitat** Often forms large, spreading colonies in rainforests and wet sclerophyll forests in damp, shady sites along the coast and tablelands from northern Qld to northeastern NSW, as far south as Dungog. **Family** Dryopteridaceae.

Lastreopsis acuminata   **Shiny Shield Fern**
(syn. *L. shepherdii*)

A small, erect fern with clustered fronds and a short-creeping rhizome clothed with dark-brown scales and densely covered with the remains of the stalks of dead fronds. **Fronds** Very variable. Tufted, erect, shiny green, arching, lanceolate to narrow-triangular in outline, 25-90 cm long and 6-30 cm wide. The fronds are bipinnately divided into many segments, and some of the lower ones may be divided again, although the terminal segments are undivided. The segments have deeply-toothed margins, a prominent central vein and unbranched or forked marginal veins. The main stalk is pale-brown and scaly towards the base. It is about the same length as the frond, ridged, with a channel on the upper surface filled with hairs and continuous with the secondary stalks. **Sporangia** Arranged in distinct, raised round clusters, 0.5-2 mm across, on the underside of the fertile leaf segments between the central vein and the margins. **Habitat** Grows in rainforests, wet sclerophyll forests and damp gullies, usually in dark areas near creeks, and sometimes in caves. This species is common along the coast and tablelands from southeastern Qld through NSW, southern Vic. to southeastern SA and Tas. **Family** Dryopteridaceae.

Angiopteris evecta   **Giant Fern**

A large fern with a thick, woody, deeply-grooved trunk to 80 cm high and 1 m diameter in older specimens, and huge, arching fronds forming a magnificent rosette. **Fronds** Glossy dark-green, up to 5 m long, with erect, arching, fleshy stalks, smooth and green with a swollen base bearing two large, ear-like bracts. The fronds are bipinnately divided into large linear to lanceolate segments with toothed or serrated margins, attached by very short stalks with swollen bases. The ultimate segments are 4-20 cm long and 15-25 mm wide, with a prominent central vein and simple or once-forked marginal veins. **Sporangia** Relatively large and arranged in oblong clusters of 4-6 pairs close to the margins of the fertile leaf segments, straddling the marginal veins. **Habitat** Grows in rainforests and wet sclerophyll forests in protected sites along the coast of Qld to about 600 m altitude, also in subtropical rainforest in the Tweed Valley of northeastern NSW, where it is very rare. **Family** Marattiaceae.

Lastreopsis munita

Angiopteris evecta

Lastreopsis acuminata

MW.

Diplazium australe
(syn. Athyrium australe)

Austral Lady Fern

A large, tufted fern to 1.6 m high, with a stout, erect rhizome covered with thick, dull black scales, often forming a short trunk. **Fronds** Bright green, semi-erect and arching, to 2 m long with a stout, fleshy stalk. The fronds are mostly bipinnately divided into numerous fine, lacy segments with toothed -margins. The lower segments are deeply-lobed and cut almost to the midrib, to give the frond a tripinnate appearance. The segments are 5-25 mm long and 2-10 mm wide with rounded tips, a prominent central vein and simple or forked lateral veins. They are attached to a light-brown secondary stalk which is green where it joins the main stalk. **Sporangia** Arranged in oblong clusters, 1-2 mm long, along the bases of the lateral veins on the underside of the fertile leaf segments. **Habitat** Grows in moist, shady sites in rainforests along the coast and tablelands from southeastern Qld through NSW, Vic. and Tas. Under ideal conditions it will grow a thick, woody trunk, resembling a tree fern. **Family** Athyriaceae.

Polystichum proliferum

Mother Shield Fern

A medium-sized to tall fern with a thick, erect rhizome becoming trunk-like with age and covered with dark-brown, shiny scales with pale margins. This species proliferates freely from the buds near the ends of the fronds which take root as the fronds age. It is very similar to the lesser-known *Polystichum australiense* (also illustrated), which can be distinguished by its dark-green fronds and dull scales. **Fronds** Light-green, turning darker with age, and spirally arranged in a crown. The fronds are erect, narrow-linear to triangular in outline, 0.5-1.3 m long and up to 30 cm wide. The main stalk is pale-brown and ridged above, with scattered hair-like scales, often giving rise to scaly buds near the apex. The fronds are mostly bipinnately divided into numerous small, lobed segments with toothed margins, the lower ones may be deeply cut to give them a tripinnate appearance. The segments are thick and leathery, to 1 cm long and 5 mm wide with a short stalk. **Sporangia** Arranged in raised round clusters about 1 mm diameter, often forming a dark-brown mass on the underside of the fertile leaf segments. **Habitat** Grows in large colonies in rainforests and sclerophyll forests, and is common and widespread along the coast and tablelands to quite high altitudes, from northern NSW to Vic., southeastern SA and Tas., with rare occurrences in the George Gill range of the NT. **Family** Dryopteridaceae.

Todea barbara

King Fern

A massive fern with an erect, black trunk, fibrous outside and covered with the broken bases of the old fronds. The trunk may grow up to 3 m tall and 1 m diameter, with several crowns of fronds. **Fronds** Erect, leathery, glossy-green above and paler below, 0.5-2.5 m long and 10-30 cm wide, including the smooth stalks which are winged and hairy at the base. The fronds are bipinnately divided into numerous closely-spaced, stalkless, lanceolate segments with toothed margins, a prominent central vein and forked lateral veins. **Sporangia** Spherical and arranged in oval or oblong masses along the lateral veins of the lower segments of the young, immature fronds, later covering most of the undersides of the segments. After releasing their green spores, the sporangia close and persist as a red-brown mass on mature fronds. **Habitat** Grows in damp sites in rocky crevices, shaded gullies, and along creek banks in sclerophyll forests and rainforests along the coast and tablelands from northeastern Qld through NSW to Vic., northern Tas., and the Mt Lofty Ranges in SA. They are slow-growing, very hardy, and thrive in damp, well-drained sites. **Family** Osmundaceae.

Diplazium australe

Polystichum proliferum

Todea barbara

Polystichum australiense

M.W.

Adiantum aethiopicum

Common Maidenhair Fern

A small, delicate fern with a long, wiry, creeping and branching rhizome covered with papery scales, suckering profusely to form a spreading clump. **Fronds** Erect or arching and slightly prostrate, triangular in outline and 10-60 cm long. The fronds are usually bipinnate, although they may be tripinnate or occasionally quadripinnate in parts. The leaf segments are thin and pale-green, heart or fan-shaped, 3-12 mm long and 3-12 mm wide. The outer margins are finely-serrated and usually lobed. The segments are borne on slender, wiry, shiny, deep reddish-brown stalks. The veins are clearly visible and fan out from the base of the segments, branching towards the outer margins. Sterile fronds are spreading, while fertile fronds are erect with smaller leaflets. **Sporangia** Arranged in kidney-shaped clusters deeply embedded in the margins of the fertile leaf segments, with 1-5 clusters on each segment. **Habitat** Grows in large colonies in moist open sites and along riverbanks, in rocky locations from tropical to temperate regions. It is one of the most common ferns, found along the coast and tablelands of Qld, NSW, Vic., eastern SA, southeastern WA and northeastern Tas. It is very adaptable and will tolerate a wide range of conditions, although strong sunlight, low temperatures and frost damage the fronds. **Family** Adiantaceae.

Adiantum cunninghamii

A tall, clumping, robust fern with numerous fronds with long, coarse stalks arising from a short-creeping and branching rhizome covered with dark-brown scales. **Fronds** Erect and spreading, usually bipinnate, although they may be tripinnate in parts; broadly triangular in outline and 10-90 cm long. The leaf segments are greyish-green with deep purple or salmon pink new growth, oblong to fan-shaped, 2-30 mm long and 2-26 mm wide, the outer margins are irregularly-toothed and often lobed. They are borne on slender, wiry, scurfy, 3-angled, grooved, dark-brown shiny stalks. The veins are clearly visible and fan out from the base of the segments to the outer margins. **Sporangia** Arranged in kidney-shaped clusters shallowly embedded in the margins of the fertile leaf segments. There are 4-10 clusters per segment, giving the appearance of a continuous brown strip around the margins. **Habitat** Grows in rainforests, mainly in highland areas above 800 m in eastern Qld, preferring shady sites on well-drained loamy soil, and resents disturbance. **Family** Adiantaceae.

Adiantum hispidulum

Rough Maidenhair Fern

A small, hardy, erect fern with numerous fronds arising from a short-creeping and branching rhizome covered with pale to dark-brown scales. **Fronds** Erect and spreading. The fronds are very variable, from bipinnate to tripinnate; 10-65 cm long with long, finger-like divisions. The leaf segments are pale to dark-green, tough, and the ultimate segments are clothed in minute, soft, white hairs; new growth is pinkish-red. The segments are rectangular to fan-shaped with toothed outer margins, 2-20 mm long, and borne on shiny, dark-brown to black, stiff, rough, angular stems, 5-30 cm long. The veins are very fine and radiate from the base of the segments to the outer margins. **Sporangia** Arranged in small, kidney-shaped clusters, deeply embedded in the margins of the fertile leaf segments. There are 3-15 clusters per segment. **Habitat** Grows in rainforests, tall wet sclerophyll forests and in shady sites in open bushland, often among rocks. This hardy species is widespread along the coast and tablelands from northeastern Qld through eastern NSW to southeastern Vic., central NT and northern WA. **Family** Adiantaceae.

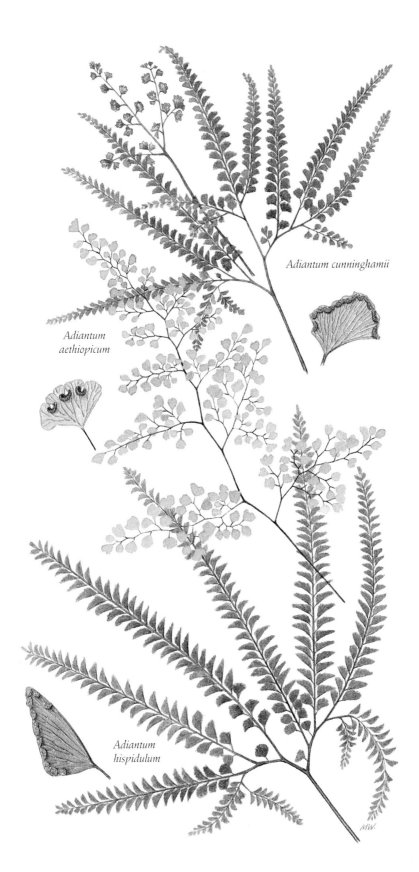

Adiantum cunninghamii

*Adiantum
aethiopicum*

*Adiantum
hispidulum*

M.W.

Hymenophyllum flabellatum
Shiny Filmy Fern

A small to medium-sized, delicate, epiphytic, filmy fern with long, arching fronds hanging from tree fern trunks and rock faces, and a very slender, long-creeping, much-branched, light-brown, wiry rhizome. Young growth is covered with pale red-brown woolly hairs. **Fronds** Pendant, pale-green, 5-35 cm long and 2-5 cm broad, thin and delicate with a thin, dark-brown stalk to 15 cm long. The fronds are bipinnately divided into irregular, deeply-lobed, flat segments with entire margins, 4-20 cm long and 15-50 mm wide. **Sporangia** Arranged in round clusters to 1.5 mm across, borne on small terminal or lateral lobes of the fertile leaf segments, slightly immersed in the margins and covered by a 2-lobed membrane. **Habitat** Grows in wet sites in subtropical and temperate rainforests and fern gullies, generally in the highlands, forming large clumps or mats on tree trunks and rocks. This species is widespread along the coast and tablelands from southeastern Qld through NSW to Vic. and Tas. **Family** Hymenophyllaceae.

Hymenophyllum cupressiforme
Common Filmy Fern

A small, delicate, filmy fern with arching fronds and a much-branched, long-creeping, wiry rhizome. Young parts are sparsely clothed with red-brown hairs. **Fronds** Dark-green, 2-9 cm long and 15-30 mm broad, thin and delicate with a very thin stalk, 5-35 mm long, often with a narrow wing on the upper part of the midrib. The fronds are usually bipinnately divided into deeply-lobed, flat, broad, finger-like segments with rounded, minutely-serrated tips. **Sporangia** Arranged in ovate or orbicular clusters about 2 mm across, borne on the margins of very short lobes at the base of the upper fertile leaf segments, covered by a membrane with minutely-toothed margins. **Habitat** Grows in moist sites in rainforests and fern gullies, forming dense mats on sheltered rock faces, tree trunks and creek banks. This species propagates readily and is common and abundant along the coast and tablelands from southeastern Qld through NSW to Vic. and Tas. **Family** Hymenophyllaceae.

Asplenium flaccidum
Weeping Spleenwort

A medium-sized to large, pendulous, usually epiphytic fern, often forming large hanging masses, with a thick, short-creeping rhizome clothed with large, dark-brown to purplish-black scales. **Fronds** Thick and leathery, to 90 cm long with a fairly short stalk, bright-green, variable, usually bipinnately divided into relatively well-spaced, narrow, oblong segments with entire or lobed margins. The segments are stalkless with free veins, drooping and 5-12 mm long. This species does not produce buds on the fronds. **Sporangia** Arranged in a single linear cluster, 2-7 mm long, along and below the vein close to the curled inner margins on the underside of the fertile leaf segments. **Habitat** Grows in rainforests and *Nothofagus* forests on rocks or trees in wet sites. This species is locally common along the coast and tablelands from southeastern Qld through eastern NSW to Vic. and Tas. **Family** Aspleniaceae.

Hymenophyllum flabellatum

Hymenophyllum cupressiforme

Asplenium flaccidum

M.W.

Cheilanthes sieberi

Mulga Fern

A small, clumping fern with a short to medium-creeping, wiry rhizome clothed with narrow, hair-like scales. **Fronds** Erect, dark-green, narrow-lanceolate or oblong in outline, usually 15-25 cm long, sometimes to 45 cm long, and 2-5 cm wide at the base with long, very slender, red-brown to dark-brown, shiny stalks. The fronds are bipinnately divided into many small, lobed segments, some of which may be cut almost to the midrib and appear tripinnate. The segments are more or less triangular with blunt tips and curled-under margins, 2-8 mm long and 1-3 mm wide. The old dead fronds may persist for years. **Sporangia** Arranged in small, rounded clusters borne on the tips of the tiny lateral veins on the underside of the fertile leaf segments, forming short lines beneath the curled margins. **Habitat** Grows among rocks, along watercourses, in gorges, dry sclerophyll forests, woodlands, scrubs, alluvial flats, rocky hillsides and rock crevices. Widespread along the coast and inland throughout Australia, Lord Howe Is. and Norfolk Is. The fronds are poisonous to cattle and sheep. **Family** Sinopteridaceae.

Lygodium microphyllum

Climbing Maidenhair Fern

A delicate, climbing fern with fronds arising in two rows on the upper surface of the rhizome, which is densely covered with short brown hairs. **Fronds** Pale-green, long and slender, reaching a length of several metres, twining around themselves and nearby vegetation and ascending towards the tree canopy. They are bipinnately divided into alternate segments with minutely-serrated margins and short stalks. The secondary leaf stalks are relatively widely spaced along the thin and wiry main stalk. They are divided into two approximately equal branches with a hairy dormant bud in the fork. There are usually 4-11 leaf segments on each secondary stalk. The sterile segments are roughly triangular or lobed, 2-5 cm long and 1-2 cm wide. Fertile segments are fan-shaped, semi-circular or triangular with lobed margins, to 15 mm long and 12 mm wide. **Sporangia** Arranged in roughly oblong clusters, 1-2 mm long, arising at the ends of the tiny marginal veins on the underside of the fertile leaf segments, and protruding like teeth from the margins. **Habitat** Grows in or near rainforests and open, swampy sites. Widespread and locally common along the coast of north-eastern WA, NT, eastern Qld and northeastern NSW as far south as Iluka. **Family** Schizaeaceae.

Microlepia speluncae

A tall, lacy, extremely variable fern with a medium-creeping, fleshy rhizome covered with short, pale hairs on the younger parts, giving rise to two closely-spaced rows of leaf stalks. **Fronds** Dull-green, semi-erect, to 1 m long, broadly triangular in outline and bipinnately divided into numerous deeply lobed segments, often cut down to the midrib to give the frond a tripinnate appearance. The main stalk is shiny dark-brown and hairy above, pale and grooved below. The leaf segments are thin-textured, paler and hairy on the underside, with sunken marginal veins on the upper surface. **Sporangia** Arranged in distinct, raised, globular clusters about 1 mm diameter, at the ends of the marginal veins at the base of the lobe divisions on the underside of the fertile leaf segments. **Habitat** Grows in rainforest margins and open forests. Widespread along the coast and table-lands of northeastern WA and northeastern Qld. **Family** Dennstaedtiaceae.

*Cheilanthes
sieberi*

*Lygodium
microphyllum*

*Microlepia
speluncae*

M.W.

Lastreopsis marginans   **Bordered or Glossy Shield Fern**

A medium-size, erect, lacy fern, with a short-creeping rhizome sparsely covered with thin, dark-brown scales, giving rise to well-spaced clumps of fronds. **Fronds** Crowded, erect, glossy dark-green, 50-115 cm long and up to 60 cm wide, broadly triangular in outline and mostly tripinnately divided into many small segments. Some of the lower segments may be divided again, while the terminal segments on the secondary stalks are undivided. The leaf segments are attached by broad bases or short stalks, they have entire or serrated margins and a prominent central vein. The main leaf stalks are hairy and ridged above. **Sporangia** Arranged in distinct, raised, round clusters in a line close to the margins of the fertile leaf segments. The leaf margins are curled over the sporangia. **Habitat** Grows in dense rainforests and wet sclerophyll forests in shady sites in both wet and dry situations. This is a hardy species, locally common along the coast and tablelands of southeastern Qld and northeastern NSW as far south as the Clarence River. **Family** Dryopteridaceae.

Adiantum formosum   **Giant Maidenhair Fern**

A large, delicate-looking fern with a much-branched, long-creeping rhizome, deeply buried and clothed in narrow brown scales, giving rise to individual, widely-spaced fronds. **Fronds** Erect, dark-green with pale-green new growth, 60-120 cm long, broadly triangular in outline and mostly tripinnately divided into many small segments, 5-15 mm long; some of the lower segments may be divided again, and the terminal segments on the secondary stalks are undivided. The stalks are shiny, deep-purple to black with minute brown hairs, and the main stalks zig-zag between the thin tertiary stalks. The leaf segments have toothed and lobed outer margins, and are attached by small stalks. They have very fine branching veins fanning out from the stalks to the outer margins. **Sporangia** Arranged in small, raised, crescent-shaped clusters on the outer margins of the fertile leaf segments, commonly with 5-9 sporangia per segment in shallow depressions. **Habitat** Grows in large colonies in moist, shady sites along stream banks in rainforests and tall eucalypt forests. This is a vigorous hardy species, widespread along the coast and tablelands from northeastern Qld through NSW to southeastern Vic. **Family** Adiantaceae.

Arachniodes aristata   **Prickly Shield Fern**

A medium-sized to tall, clumping fern forming spreading patches and arising from a long-creeping rhizome densely-clothed with papery brown scales. **Fronds** Glossy dark-green, leathery and prickly, to 120 cm long on long stalks, broadly triangular in outline and mostly tripinnately divided into many small segments. Some of the lower segments may be divided again, and the terminal segments on the secondary stalks are undivided. The leaf segments are mostly attached by small stalks. They have sharply pointed tips, toothed margins and a sunken central vein. **Sporangia** Arranged in distinct, raised, round clusters on each side of the central veins of the fertile leaf segments. **Habitat** Grows in tropical and subtropical rainforests and open woodlands, usually near creeks, forming dense colonies. This slow-growing hardy species is common along the coast and tablelands from northeastern Qld to central eastern NSW. **Family** Dryopteridaceae.

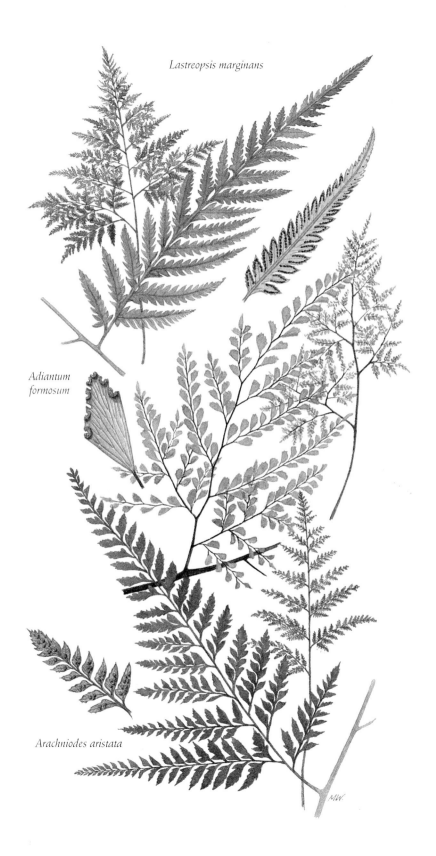

Lastreopsis marginans

Adiantum formosum

Arachniodes aristata

MW

Pteridium esculentum

Common Bracken

A tall, coarse fern with a long-creeping, much-branched, woody rhizome, 2-10 mm diameter and up to 1.5 m long, covered with dark red hairs and giving rise to stout leaf stalks. **Fronds** Stiffly erect, dark-green, broadly triangular in outline, 0.6-3 m long including the brown stalks, and tripinnately divided into numerous segments. The lower segments are deeply lobed and often divided again, the ultimate segments are linear or oblong. The segments are coarse and leathery with short, fine hairs below, while the upper surface may have a few reddish hairs near the margins. All have a small lobe at the base. The leaf stalks are grooved on the upper surface and the midribs may have a few dark red hairs. **Sporangia** Arranged in continuous linear clusters below the curled-under margins of the fertile leaf segments. **Habitat** Grows in abundance in a wide variety of habitats on well-drained soils in dry sclerophyll forests, damp, sandy flats, sandstone gullies, at the edge of sand dunes and in pastures. Poisonous to stock and often considered a weed. Very common and widespread along the coast, tablelands and inland slopes of Qld, NSW, Vic., SA, Tas. and southwestern WA. **Family** Dennstaedtiaceae.

Davallia pyxidata

Hare's Foot Fern

A medium-sized to tall, epiphytic fern, growing on rocks or trees, with a long-creeping, branching, thick and fleshy rhizome to 12 mm diameter, covered with brown, papery scales and bearing two scattered rows of deciduous leaf stalks 10-20 cm long. **Fronds** Glossy-green above and paler below, broadly triangular in outline, 30-100 cm long and up to 25 cm wide, tripinnately divided into numerous small, lobed segments, some of the lower ones may be further divided. The segments are leathery and asymmetrical at the base, with free or once-forked veins visible on the undersides. The fertile segments are narrower with small marginal bulges on the upper surface. **Sporangia** Arranged in distinct tubular clusters about 1 mm long on the margins of the underside of the fertile leaf segments, causing a bulge on the upper surface. **Habitat** A hardy species growing on tree trunks in rainforests and climbing over rocks in dry sclerophyll forests. Widespread and locally common along the coast and tablelands in Qld, NSW and southwestern Vic. **Family** Davalliaceae.

Davallia denticulata

A medium-sized to tall fern, growing on the ground or over rocks and on trees, with a medium-creeping, thick and fleshy rhizome covered with light-brown scales and giving rise to two rows of fronds. **Fronds** Erect, to 1 m long, broadly triangular in outline and tripinnately divided into many small, deeply lobed segments. Some of the lower ones may be further divided to give the frond a quadripinnate appearance in parts. The main stalk has a zig-zag shape. The segments have a prominent central vein and free or once-forked marginal veins. The fertile segments are finer than the sterile ones. **Sporangia** Arranged in distinct oblong to cup-shaped clusters on each lobe on the margins of the undersides of the fertile leaf segments. **Habitat** A hardy species growing in exposed sites along the coast and tablelands of northeastern Qld, usually on the ground, although it also grows over rocks and on tree trunks in rainforests. **Family** Davalliaceae.

Pteridium
esculentum

Davallia
denticulata

Davallia
pyxidata

Dennstaedtia davallioides   **Lacy Ground Fern**

A tall, spreading fern with delicate, lacy fronds and a long-creeping, tough and woody rhizome,
3-5 mm diameter, densely clothed with short red-brown hairs. **Fronds** Erect with drooping tips,
dark-green, soft and thin, to 1.6 m tall and 50 cm wide with shiny, reddish-brown stalks, grooved
above and clothed with reddish-brown hairs near the base. The fronds are tripinnately divided into
many small, deeply lobed segments, some of which may be further divided to give the frond a
quadripinnate appearance in parts. The leaf segments are up to 1 cm long with a prominent midvein and free or once-forked marginal veins. **Sporangia** Arranged in distinct, raised, round
clusters, to 1 mm diameter, on the margins at the apex or the base of the lobes on the underside of
the fertile leaf segments. **Habitat** Grows in rainforest gullies, cool, shady sites and along creeks
in alluvial flats and wet sclerophyll forests. This species is widespread and commonly found along
the coast and tablelands from southern Qld to the central coast of NSW, Vic. and Norfolk Island.
Family Dennstaedtiaceae.

Oenotrichia tripinnata   **Hairy Lace Fern**

A small, clumping fern with erect, finely-divided fronds arising from a short-creeping rhizome
clothed with dark reddish hairs. **Fronds** Fine and lacy, dark-green, broadly triangular in outline,
up to 50 cm tall including the dull-green, wiry stalks which are clothed with white hairs. The
fronds are generally tripinnately divided into many small, thin-textured, curved, lobed segments
with short stalks and forked veins. The upper part of the frond may have a bipinnate appearance
with deeply-lobed segments. **Sporangia** Arranged in small, raised, round clusters along the
margins of the fertile leaf segments at the ends of the veinlets, with one cluster per lobe.
Habitat Grows in moist, shady sites, often on rock faces near creeks in rainforests. This slow-
growing species is restricted to the highlands and tablelands of northeastern Qld. **Family**
Dennstaedtiaceae.

Calochlaena dubia   **Common Ground Fern**
(syn Culcita dubia)

A tall, spreading fern with tough, lacy fronds and a stout, long-creeping, branched rhizome, 8-
25 mm diameter, clothed with soft, silvery hairs intermixed with golden-yellow hairs. **Fronds**
Pale to yellowish-green, broadly triangular in outline, erect with drooping tips, 40-150 cm tall,
including the yellow-brown stalks which are 30-80 cm long. The fronds are tripinnately divided
into many small, deeply-lobed segments up to 1 cm long with broad bases, the lower ones may be
further divided to give them a quadripinnate appearance. **Sporangia** Arranged in raised, round
clusters, 8-15 mm diameter, on the underside of the fertile leaf segments, close to the margins
which are partially folded over them. There are up to 20 clusters per segment, positioned at the
ends of the veins. **Habitat** Grows in very large colonies on forested slopes, open gullies and
creek flats, usually on poor soils. A very hardy and adaptable species, widespread and very common along the coast and tablelands of eastern Australia from northern Qld through NSW to Vic.
and Tas. **Family** Dicksoniaceae.

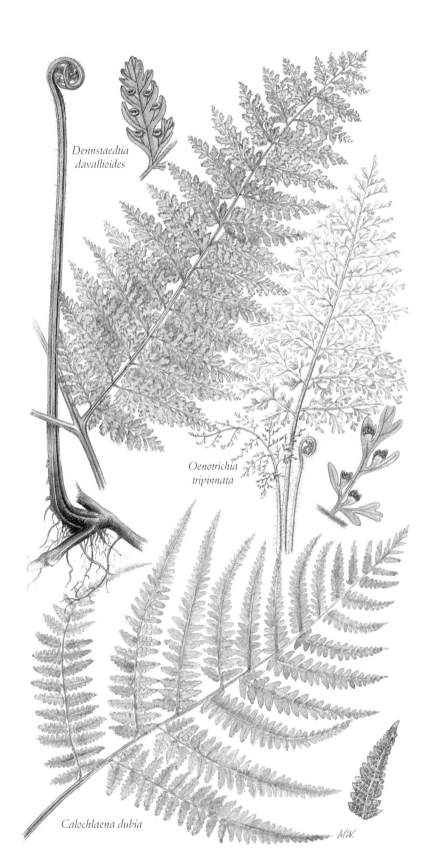

Dennstaedtia davallioides

Oenotrichia tripinnata

Calochlaena dubia

M.W.

Cyathea australis

The Rough Tree Fern is a tall, slender tree fern, widespread and common along the east coast of Australia from the subtropics to the cooler temperate areas. This species has a massive, rough trunk topped by a widely-spreading crown of large, arching, finely-divided, dull, dark-green fronds.

Trunk Dark-brown, rough and fibrous, 2.5-20 m tall and 16-40 cm diameter. In older specimens the trunk is often thickened at the base by masses of wiry adventitious roots. It is covered in the upper part and almost to the base by the short, hard, woody and pointed remains of the old leaf bases. Glossy reddish-brown scales, 2-5 cm long, stiff and often twisted with pale fragile margins, cover the leaf bases and the upper part of the trunk.

Fronds Broadly ovate in outline, 2-5 m long and 45-100 cm across. They are dark-green above, paler to whitish-green below, and often bleached in sunny sites. The fronds are tripinnately divided into numerous small segments with serrated or shallowly-lobed margins. The smallest leaf segments are thin and leathery, sickle-shaped, 4-13 mm long and 2-4 mm wide with a prominent central vein and forked lateral veins clothed with short hairs. The lowest pairs of segments on the secondary leaf stalks may be shortly stalked, while the remainder are stalkless or joined at their bases. The ultimate segments unite to form long, lobed tips at the ends of the secondary leaf stalks. The main stalk is quite short, to 60 cm long, dark-brown and densely covered with coarsely-pointed conical spines at the base. The base is 1-3 cm broad and covered with glossy light-brown, narrow-lanceolate scales, 2-5 cm long.

Sporangia Arranged in distinct, raised, round clusters on the underside of the fertile leaf segments. They are about 1 mm diameter and partially covered with a semicircular series of thin, fawn-coloured scales. There are usually 3-8 pairs of sporangia per segment, situated at the forks of the lateral veins away from the margins of the leaf segments.

Habitat Grows in rainforest gullies and open forests on hillsides in moist, shady sites. The Rough Tree Fern is probably the most common tree fern in southeastern Australia. A very hardy species, its range extends from the coast to inland montane areas at around 1200 m altitude. It will tolerate full sun as long as plenty of water is available, and is easily grown, although young, developing fronds may be damaged by frost.

Distribution Widespread and common along the coast and tablelands from southeastern Qld through NSW to Vic. and Tas.

Family Cyatheaceae.

Cyathea cooperi

Cooper's, Scaly or Straw Tree Fern

Cooper's Tree Fern is a tall, slender tree fern found along the east coast of Australia, particularly in highland areas, from temperate to tropical regions. It has a distinctively patterned trunk and large, pale-green, finely-divided fronds that form a graceful, spreading crown of around 13-18 fronds, with a number of very attractive, curled, new fronds covered with long, silky, whitish scales emerging from the centre.

Trunk Dark greyish-brown, to 12 m tall and 15 cm diameter. The trunk is hard and woody, thickened at the base, and covered with a distinctive pattern of fairly large, smooth, clean-cut, oval leaf scars. The old leaf bases do not persist on the trunk.

Fronds Dull light-green above and slightly paler below, up to 5 m long and 22-130 cm wide, broadly ovate in outline and abruptly narrowed towards the tip. The fronds are tripinnately divided into numerous small, alternate, stalkless leaf segments. The segments are thin and leathery, 4-17 mm long and 1-4 mm wide, broadly sickle-shaped to oblong with a rounded tip and fine, irregularly-serrated margins, rarely lobed. Each secondary leaf stalk bears 10-23 (usually 16-20) pairs of segments, joined to the leaf stalk by their broad bases. Larger specimens may have stalked segments towards the base of the frond. The segments have a central vein and small, forked lateral veins. The main leaf stalks are light yellowish-brown or brown, to 50 cm or more long and 8-30 mm wide. They are deeply grooved on the upper surface and bear small, dark-brown, warty protuberances 0.2-0.5 mm across. Their bases are covered with silky, whitish, linear scales, 2-5 cm long and 0.5-5 mm wide, interspersed with smaller, reddish-brown scales, 5-15 mm long and up to 0.5 mm wide.

Sporangia Arranged in raised, round clusters on the underside of the fertile leaf segments. They are 0.5-1 mm diameter and surrounded by a ring of chestnut-coloured scales. Each leaf segment usually bears 1-10 pairs of sporangia clusters, located on the forks of the lateral veins quite close to the central vein.

Habitat Grows in moist gullies in protected sites in warm coastal rainforests and open forests, often on mountain slopes near creeks. Cooper's Tree Ferns are fast growing, hardy, and will recover from frosts. They are easy to grow and very popular in cultivation.

Distribution Widespread and common along the coast from northeastern Qld to southeastern NSW as far south as Durras Mt. This is the most common tree fern in northeastern Qld.

Family Cyatheaceae.

Cyathea leichhardtiana

Prickly Tree Fern

The Prickly Tree Fern is a small to medium-sized, slender tree fern found along the east coast of Australia from subtropical to temperate areas. The glossy dark-green fronds emerge from the top of the trunk to form a spreading crown. The bases of the arching leaf stalks are covered with very sharp woody spines, and the young, curled-up developing fronds are clothed with light-brown scales.

Trunk Dark-brown, straight and slender, 1-7 m high and 5-15 cm diameter. Most of the old black bases of the leaf stalks persist on the trunk, and these are covered with vicious thorns. In older specimens the lower part of the trunk often sheds the leaf bases to leave smooth, widely spaced leaf scars.

Fronds Shiny dark-green above and paler below, broadly ovate in outline, to 3 m long and 70 cm wide. The fronds are tripinnately divided into numerous small, stalkless leaf segments, attached to pale-brown grooved midribs with small spines on the lower surface. The segments are oblong to slightly sickle-shaped with toothed or finely serrated margins, 2-20 mm long and 1-5 mm wide, alternately arranged with usually 12-26 pairs along the midrib, joined by their broad bases. The ultimate segments are united to form a narrow, lobed tail. Larger specimens may have stalked lower segments with lobed margins. They have a central vein and small, forked lateral veins clothed with yellowish-white scales. The main leaf stalks are reddish-brown to purplish-black and deeply grooved on the upper surface. Their bases are armed with black or dark reddish-brown, sharply-pointed, curved or straight thorns, 1-4 mm long, and bear tufts of narrow, silky, whitish scales 0.5-6 cm long.

Sporangia Arranged in raised, round clusters, 0.3-0.8 mm diameter, on the underside of the fertile leaf segments, situated on the forks of the lateral veins quite close to the central vein. There are usually 2-12 pairs of clusters per segment, becoming confluent in the later stages of their development. They are covered by a pale fawn-coloured, silky membrane that soon breaks into fragments.

Habitat Grows in moist gullies in protected sites in rainforests and open forests, often on mountain slopes along the banks of creeks, often forming pure stands. They are slow growing and may be damaged by heavy frosts, and prefer well-drained soil in partial shade.

Distribution Widespread and fairly common along the coast and tablelands from the Eungella Range in northeastern Qld through eastern NSW to the far eastern corner of Vic.

Family Cyatheaceae.

Cyathea rebeccae

This attractive species is a medium-sized, very slender tree fern found in lowland and highland rainforests of northeastern Australia. It has a loose, spreading crown of usually 8 large, glossy, dark-green arching fronds clothed with scales, with a few slender new fronds emerging from the centre of the crown. New plants sometimes grow from underground stems around the base of the plant.

Trunk Dark-brown, 2-7 m tall and 2.5-10 cm diameter. The trunk is fibrous at the base, woody above, and retains the leaf bases to at least half way down the trunk. Below this the trunk has oval leaf scars, and bears a few adventitious roots around the thickened base.

Fronds Dark shiny-green and slightly paler below, 2-3 m long and up to 1.2 m wide, broadly ovate in outline and arching gently. The fronds are bipinnately divided into numerous alternate segments with short stalks and entire or serrated margins. There are 9-35 pairs of segments, fairly widely spaced along the primary stalks. The segments are 25-85 mm long and 6-20 mm wide, narrow-lanceolate to ovate or oblong with a long, pointed tip, except for the lower segments which often have broadly rounded tips. They have a prominent central vein and branching lateral veins. Sterile segments are broader than the fertile ones. The main leaf stalks of the fronds are reddish-purple, cylindrical and held close to the trunk at the base. They are grooved above, have 2 rows of oval pits and small, rough, rounded projections. The stalks are covered with fawn, flattened, papery scales, and the bases bear brownish-purple, thick and glossy linear scales, 7-15 mm long, with broad bases and fawn margins.

Sporangia Arranged in distinct, well-raised, orbicular clusters, 0.75-1.25 mm diameter, on the underside of the fertile leaf segments, sited at the forks of the lateral veins away from the margins. The clusters are crowded in 2 irregular rows along each side of the central veins of the segments, the inner row is situated on the outer branchlets of the veins, the outer row on the inner branchlets.

Habitat Grows in gullies and along ridges in lowland and highland rainforests from sea level to over 1500 m altitude, preferring damp sites along creek banks on decomposed basalt and granite soils. This species is slow-growing but easy to grow, and requires a shady site with protection from frost in southern areas.

Distribution Abundant along the coast and tablelands of central eastern and northeastern Qld, extending into Flores.

Family Cyatheaceae.

Cyathea woollsiana

This very attractive tree fern is found in the highland rainforests of northeastern Australia. It is medium-sized, fairly stout, with a wide, spreading crown of broad, bright-green, arching fronds arising from the top of the trunk, with a few curled new fronds densely covered with long fawn scales emerging from the centre of the crown.

Trunk Fairly stout and erect, to 7 m tall and 25 cm diameter. The trunk is fibrous at the base and more woody above, and covered with persistent rough frond bases. These may have a group of curved spines on the lower surface, and are covered with bristly brown or black scales. Older specimens shed the leaf bases on the lower part of the trunk to leave clean, widely-spaced leaf scars.

Fronds Bright-green above and paler to whitish-green below, broadly ovate in outline and tripinnately divided into numerous small segments with finely serrated margins. The whole frond may be up to 2.5 m long and 1.3 m wide, thin-textured and fairly soft with overlapping, crowded segments. The leaf segments are 5-15 mm long and 2-5 mm wide, oblong to slightly sickle shaped with a rounded tip, and joined to the midrib by their wide bases, although in some specimens they are fused at their bases to give the frond a bipinnate appearance with large, deeply-lobed segments. The basal pair may have very short stalks, and the terminal leaflets are fused at their bases to form a lobed, pointed tail. The leaf segments have a prominent midvein with a few hair-like scales below, and 6-10 pairs of forked lateral veins. The main stalk is deeply-grooved above, bright yellowish-brown, covered with rough, dark-brown nodules 1-3 mm long, and sparsely clothed with flattened, fawn scales. The base is dark reddish-brown, rough, and sometimes clothed with thick, woody, dark-brown spines, 15-25 mm long, covered with rusty powder at their bases. The secondary stalks are yellowish-brown to reddish-brown, with reddish-brown hairs above.

Sporangia Arranged in distinct, raised, round clusters about 1 mm across on the underside of the fertile leaf segments. They are located close to the midvein at the forks in the small lateral veins, or a short distance along the veins. There are 1-7 pairs of clusters per leaf segment, each is partially covered by a thin, tissue-like hemispherical cover.

Habitat Grows in rainforests and open forests along creeks in shaded sites, usually at higher elevations. It is hardy although slightly frost tender, and will grow in tropical and temperate areas in well-drained soil.

Distribution Endemic to the coastal ranges of northeastern Qld, and cultivated as far south as Melbourne.

Family Cyatheaceae.

Dicksonia antarctica

Soft Tree Fern

The Soft Tree Fern is a tall, stout tree fern found along the east coast of Australia and New Zealand, from subtropical to temperate areas. The large arching fronds form a spreading crown, with curled new leaves unrolling together in groups of up to 40 at one time to produce spectacular flushes of new growth. The unfurled young fronds and their stalks are covered with long, soft, reddish-brown hairs.

Trunk Dark-brown, thick and solid, erect, to 15 m tall and 50 cm diameter, and sometimes buttressed at the base in very large, leaning specimens. The trunk is soft and fibrous, densely covered with dark reddish-brown hairs towards the crown, and covered with fibrous roots towards the base. The bases of dead fronds are retained on the upper part of the trunk.

Fronds Dark-green above and pale-green below, broadly ovate in outline and tripinnately divided into numerous small segments with lobed or serrated margins. The whole frond is 1-4.5 m long, harsh in texture, stiff, and covered with fine hairs when developing. Leaf segments are leathery, 2-5 mm long, oblong to broad ovate, with curled-under margins, stalkless or with very short stalks. The terminal segments are joined together to form a pointed tail. The leaf segments have a network of a few slightly forked yellow veins. Fertile segments are more rounded with serrated margins. The main leaf stalk is green to yellowish-brown, short, to 30 cm long, smooth, and its base is covered with long, pointed, soft, red-brown hairs, 2-4 cm long. The upper part of the stalk may also bear a few hairs.

Sporangia Arranged in prominent, raised, round clusters about 1 mm across. These are located along the margins of the fertile leaf segments at the ends of the small lateral veins, and are protected by a 2-lipped cup, one side of which is formed by the curled margin of the leaf segment, and the other side by a tissue-like cover. When the spores are ripe the protective cover breaks away from the top allowing the sporangia to release the spores.

Habitat Grows in rainforests and the wet, cooler forests of eastern Australia, preferring deep shady gullies and creek banks, where it often forms large colonies. The massive fibrous trunks host a number of epiphytes, such as orchids and smaller ferns, and possums often live in their dense crowns. This tree fern is very popular in cultivation, being quite hardy and able to tolerate drier situations, although it needs plenty of water in hot weather. It is easily transplanted, the trunk is sawn through at ground level and the expanded fronds removed. A new root system develops when planted in moist, friable soil in a shady position.

Distribution Very common along the coast and tablelands from southeastern Qld through NSW to Vic. and Tas. Soft Tree Ferns used to occur naturally in scattered locations in southeastern SA, but are now apparently extinct in this State in the wild.

Family Dicksoniaceae.

Dicksonia youngiae   **Bristly Tree Fern**

The Bristly Tree Fern is a medium-sized, relatively slender tree fern growing in the highland rain-forests of tropical and subtropical eastern Australia. This particularly attractive species is unfortunately becoming rare due to clearing of its natural habitat. It has bright-green arching fronds with coarse reddish bristles along the stems, forming a distinctive, widely-spreading crown with a mass of tangled red hairs. The unfurled young fronds are covered with fine, reddish-brown hairs.

Trunk Erect in the upper part, although the base may be prostrate. Trunks lean and fall easily. They grow to 5 m tall and 10-20 cm diameter, are dark reddish-brown, covered by the persistent leaf bases, with reddish, bristly hairs on the upper part and matted with fibrous roots towards the base. Plantlets develop on the trunk and grow noticeably when the trunk leans or falls over, taking root when they touch the ground, forming new plants.

Fronds Coarse in texture, glossy-green above and dull, pale-green below, becoming deeper green when mature. Fronds are broadly ovate in outline and tripinnately divided into numerous, closely-spaced or overlapping stalkless segments. The whole frond is 1-3 m long with main stalks up to half the length of the frond. The base of the main stalk is smooth and covered with stiff, reddish-brown bristly hairs which extend along the smaller, dark reddish-brown leaf stalks. Leaf segments are 2-6 mm long, oblong with rounded or pointed tips and slightly lobed margins, and are attached by their broad bases to pale, slightly hairy midribs. They have a network of a few, slightly forked yellow veins. The ultimate segments become smaller and are united to give the ends of the leaf stalks a bipinnate appearance, with deeply-lobed segments and a pointed tip. The margins of the fertile leaf segments are more deeply lobed.

Sporangia Arranged in very prominent raised, large, round to ovate clusters, 2-3 mm across, on the underside of the fertile leaf segments. The clusters are located at the ends of the lateral veins along the margins of the segments, and are protected on the outer side by a 2-valved cap formed by the curled margin of the leaf segment. A tissue-like cover protects the inner side.

Habitat Grows in moist sheltered sites, often along creek banks, in open forests and rainforests at higher altitudes in the tropics and subtropics, frequently forming colonies. This is a fast growing species and will grow in temperate areas in frost-free sites.

Distribution Restricted occurrences in the coastal mountains and tablelands from the Atherton Tablelands in Qld to northeastern NSW as far south as the Bellinger River.

Family Dicksoniaceae.

Glossary of terms

alternate arranged one by one along a stem, not opposite.

annual completing its life cycle in one year.

anther the top end of the stamen, bearing pollen.

aquatic growing in water.

armed bearing spines, thorns or prickles.

aromatic fragrant flowers or foliage.

ascending growing upwards.

axil the upper angle between leaf and stem or branch.

axillary arising from the axil.

bark outer covering of the stem or root.

beak pointed projection.

berry succulent non-opening fruit, usually rounded usually with many seeds.

biennial completing its life cycle in 2 years.

bipinnate a leaf twice pinnately divided.

bisexual bearing both male and female sexual organs in the same flower.

blade the expanded part of a leaf.

bract modified leaf often at the base of a flower or stem.

branchlet a small branch.

bristle short stiff hair.

bulbous swollen or bulb-shaped.

calyx outer whorl of the flower, consisting of sepals.

canopy the foliage cover.

capsule dry opening fruit of more than one carpel.

carpel female part of the flower usually comprising stigma, style and ovary.

cirrus a whip-like climbing structure arising from the ends of the leaves and bearing recurved hooks.

clasping partly or wholly surrounding the stem.

compound consisting of several similar parts.

compressed flattened.

cone a globular collection of fruits around a central axis, surrounded by woody bracts.

conical cone-shaped.

constricted drawn together, narrowed as between seeds in a pod.

creeping remaining close to the ground.

crown the leafy head of a tree.

crownshaft the cylindrical tightly packed tubular leaf bases terminating the trunk in some palms.

deciduous liable to be shed at a certain time.

decumbent lying on the ground with the tip turned up.

decussate leaves arranged opposite in pairs at right angles.

depressed flattened or sunken.

downy with short soft hairs.

drupe fleshy non-opening fruit with a hard kernel and solitary seed.

elliptical a plane surface shaped like an ellipse.

elongate extended in length.

entire undivided, without teeth or lobes.

epiphyte a plant growing on another plant or object, using it for support and not nourishment.

family a group of closely related genera.

filament stalk bearing the anther.

flagellum a whip-like climbing structure arising from a leaf axil and bearing curved hooks.

floral leaves leaves immediately below the flowers.

flower sexual reproductive structure.

follicle a dry fruit formed from 1 carpel and splitting open along the inner margin.

frond leaf of a palm or fern.

fruit seed-bearing part of a plant.

fused joined together.

genus a group of closely related species.

germinationm the growth of a seed or spore to produce a new plant.

gland embedded or projecting structure usually secreting oil, nectar, resin or water.

globular globe-shaped, spherical or nearly so.

habitat natural abode of a plant.

head dense cluster of flowers or fruits.

heath an area occupied mainly by low, shrubby plants, whose growth is conditioned by severe environmental factors.

inflorescence the flowering structure of a plant.

lanceolate lance-shaped, tapering at each end, broadest below the middle, about four times as long as broad.

lateral on the side or edge.

leaf usually a green flat organ attached to the stem, manufacturing food.

leaflet a secondary part of a compound leaf.

linear long and narrow.

littoral near the sea.

lobe rounded or pointed division of a leaf; the sepal or petal of a flower.

mallee Eucalypts growing with several stunted stems, common in arid and alpine areas.

mangrove species of plants growing in salty water along coasts and estuaries.

margin edge.

membranous thin, flexible and sheet-like.

midrib main vein of a leaf, leaflet or segment, running from base to tip.

nut a dry non-opening fruit with one seed and hard woody covering.

oblong having roughly parallel sides, longer than broad with a rounded tip.

obovate almost ovate, but broader towards the tip.

opposite in pairs one at each side of the stem.

orbicular more or less circular in outline.

ovate egg-shaped, broadest below the middle.

ovary female structure enclosing the unfertilised seeds.

ovoid an egg-shaped solid body.

ovule the body in the ovary which becomes the seed after fertilisation.

palmate a leaf divided into three or more leaflets or lobes arising from a common point.

panicle a much-branched inflorescence.

perennial a plant living for more than two years.

petal a segment of the inner whorl of the floral lobes.

pinnate a compound leaf with leaflets on opposite side of a common leaf stalk.

pistil female reproductive organ in a flower.

pod dry, opening, multi-seeded fruit.

pollen powdery substance produced in the anthers.

prostrate lying on the ground.

prop roots roots growing down from a trunk or branch and supporting the tree.

raceme an infloresence with stalked flowers borne along an unbranched axis.

rainforest a closed forest dominated by trees with soft leaves.

regular radially symmetrical.

rhizome a stem which is usually underground, producing new shoots and roots.

riverine situated beside a river.

scale a thin, dry, papery structure, a very small rudimentary leaf, or flat closely pressed leaf.

scattered leaves arranged in a random manner along the stem.

sclerophyll plants with harsh-textured, tough leaves.

scrambling climbing with the help of backward-pointing hooked spines.

scurfy bearing small, flattened, papery scales.

scrub a community dominated by shrubs.

segment a subdivision of a divided or dissected leaf or other structure.

sepal a segment of the outer whorl of the flower.

serrate a leaf margin with many sharp teeth, as on a saw.

shrub a woody, perennial plant with several stems growing from the base, without a single trunk as in a tree.

silky covered with fine soft hair.

spathulate shaped like a spatula, tapering from a rounded tip to a narrow base.

species a group of individual plants essentially alike when grown under similar conditions, normally breeding freely with others of their own kind the basic unit of biological classification.

spherical in the form of a globe.

spike a compact inflorescence of stalkless flowers.

spine a sharp, rigid structure.

sporangia spore cases.

spore a reproductive cell without an embryo.

stamen male part of a flower comprising filament and anther.

stigma receptive tip of the style.

style stalk arising from the ovary and bearing the stigma.

succulent soft and juicy.

sucker a shoot arising from the trunk or roots below ground level.

synonym (syn.) a plant name set aside in favour of an earlier one.

tepal petal or sepal, being scarcely distinguishable from each other.

terminal at the apex.

terrestrial plants growing in the ground, not aquatic or epiphytic.

tessellated in the form of small squares. tree a perennial plant with a single woody trunk and distinct head or crown.

twining climbing by coiling the stem around the support.

tufted stems or leaves growing close together.

unisexual of one sex only.

valve a cell or compartment in a fully matured capsule.

vein visible appearance of vascular tissue in a leaf.

whorl a group of three or more structures encircling an axis at the same level.

woolly having long, soft, matted hair.

Leaf shapes

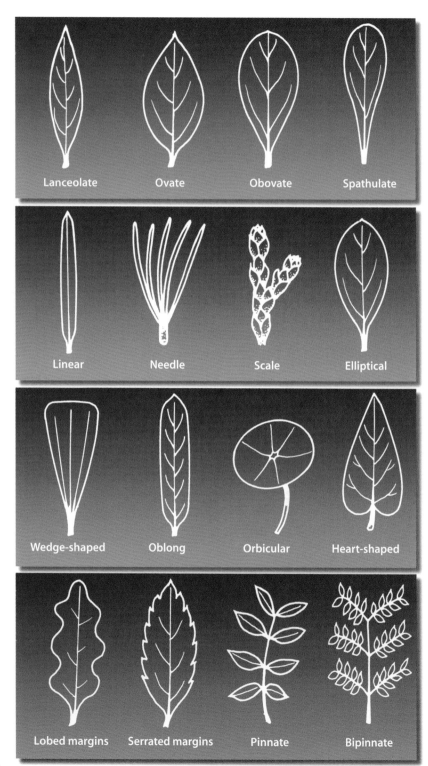

Lanceolate   Ovate   Obovate   Spathulate

Linear   Needle   Scale   Elliptical

Wedge-shaped   Oblong   Orbicular   Heart-shaped

Lobed margins   Serrated margins   Pinnate   Bipinnate

Flower parts and leaf arrangements

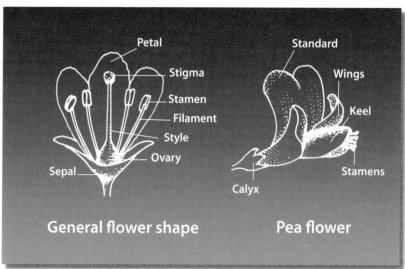

General flower shape   Pea flower

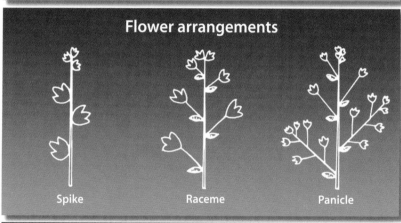

Flower arrangements

Spike   Raceme   Panicle

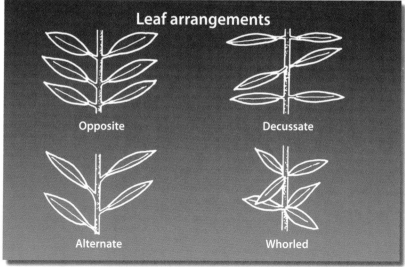

Leaf arrangements

Opposite   Decussate

Alternate   Whorled

Index